A CAMERAMAN'S

TALE

KARL COATES

Matador
9 Priory Business Park
Kibworth Beauchamp
Leicestershire LE8 0RX, UK
Tel: (+44) 116 279 2299
Fax: (+44) 116 279 2277
Email: books@troubador.co.uk
Web: www.troubador.co.uk/matador

ISBN 978 1780885 438

British Library Cataloguing in Publication Data.
A catalogue record for this book is available from the British Library.

Typeset in Aldine by Troubador Publishing Ltd
Printed and bound in the UK by TJ International, Padstow, Cornwall

Matador is an imprint of Troubador Publishing Ltd

MIX
Paper from
responsible sources
FSC® C013056

To Julia, Jordan and Kieran

Contents

Contents

Intro

I have been with Sky News for as near as dammit half my life and before that with the BBC. In the words of the White Stripes "everyone has a story to tell" and this is mine, well some of it anyway.

Having never written a book before, I was at first quite unsure what to do and how to do it. Maybe I should have turned up for a few more English lessons at school!

In the end I decided to open up a couple of cans and see what happened. What you are about to read is what came out. I have tried to tell the stories as though I was with the lads, sitting round a table in the Black Bull, as we do, and yes, at times I fly off on tangents.

Some of the tales made no bloody sense when I re-read them the morning after, so I've started over again – sober!

I have also noticed at this point that I keep getting robbed – someone is obviously watching me write and helping themselves to vast amounts of Stella from my fridge whilst I create.

I have tried to tell the stories as I remember them and put them in to some sort of time line of my life. I have pretty much given up on boring stuff like dates and times, and sometimes names, due to the fact I can't remember, but the details are true.

Some stories are long and some just a few pages, most have an amusing side to them and some not, but need to be included and will become obvious why later.

I have not set out to embarrass or upset anyone in any way, except for my brother, and I apologize in advance to anyone who feels differently. The opinions in this book are mine, and mine alone, and do not reflect the opinions of any company or organisations that I have worked for.

As I still have a job at Sky News and want to keep it, anything that appears illegal, stupid, dangerous or just damn right pathetic was all done at my time at the Beeb and not whilst at Sky.

If the Old Bill turn up I will deny everything and say I just made it up. (So that's sorted). I have no cash either so don't bother suing, and the house is in the wife's name.

Having farted on about writing a book for some time now, even before people ask "what's it about" they want to know if they're in it. Well, some are and some aren't. I could write a book about people who want to be in my book, but you just all can't be, so sorry.

You know who you are and yes a promise is a promise I will buy you beer if it's bestseller. If it isn't then I'm quids in, (that's one of those tangents I was on about).

I will try and give you the growing up part as quickly as I can, cos I know I always skip that part and want to get straight into the main course.

I was born in God's own country, Middlesbrough, in Boro General 1967, 22 years after the end of the Second World War, so that makes me very old at 43. I have two boys Jordan 15, and Kieran 14, and just the one wife Jue, (younger than me).

(For those of you that have young kids, let me tell you, wait till they hit puberty – girls and parties, no means yes and deadlines and coming in times are for wankers, and for those who have been through it unscathed well, well done).

Our rock is Julia, but known as Jue, a teenage sweetheart that I later married who keeps all our shit together, God knows how, and is a very loving caring person who has put up with a lot, believe you me.

Our happy family is completed with our crazy psycho white-haired German Shepherd, Tuco, whose name is taken from the film The Good, The Bad and The Ugly. Tuco is all three.

As for wider family, there's my brother John, also a cameraman, his missus Karen and two kids Louis and Beth. My mum Elaine is working in Canada. My dad Les is also a cameraman. His wife is Sybs. I have a step sister Lisa and her little fella Ethan and that's it. I am very lucky and I love them all dearly.

Les is my biological father but I have always known him as Les. In fact, both my kids call Julia Jue. It must be a Coatesy thing.

I was brought up in a small village on Teesside, went to a really crap private school, then on to sixth form to re-sit my O Levels, crashed out at 17 and started work. I was on Middlesbrough FC's books for a while and swam for the County.

The story really starts at 17 when I started with Les at the BBC. I started off carrying Les's tripod, and soon afterwards, I was promoted to sound recordist.

At 19 I went to live and work in Newcastle with my old mate Shaun Johnson. I was still working for the BBC, and then we spent six months with TV AM, during their strike, being a scab and earning a shed load of dosh. When the cash ran out we went back to the Beeb.

At 22 I went travelling round the world for a year, I believe they now call it a gap year. At 23 I started as a cameraman with Sky News, eight months after they first went on air.

I took over from my brother John, or Jonny as he is called in the family, and now I'm in my 21st year with them.

Later on, some ages and times don't add up, that's intentional, and not because I'm too bloody lazy to do my research properly.

My whole life has been in or around the news industry. Les is a cameraman, my brother is a cameraman, my best mate Baz is a cameraman, the lads I go on holiday with are cameramen and if they're not cameramen, they're producers, reporters or editors, except for Kev, who's a probation officer.

A night out with us if you're not in the industry is a very boring night, cos as soon as the beers flow, so do the stories and for sure all my mates have a book in them too.

Even as a little boy I can always remember not being able to get at the milk in the fridge for all the cans of film that were stored there, and of being taken on jobs to meet the likes of the Two Ronnies or eating crisps in press boxes at football matches, or watching ships being launched, cooling towers being blown up or feeding pit ponies or being told you'll never see this again.

No one knows the North East better than we do. We really have been there, seen it, done it…sometimes on a global scale. What we do and what we still do is record history and that can't be a bad job, in fact it's the best job in the world.

Sorry Mrs President

When Jimmy Carter was President of The United States of America, he came to Newcastle with a load of fellow Americans and set up the Friendship Force. As well as drinking Brown Ale and learning Geordie, he and his American chums were hosted by Brits with similar backgrounds, jobs and families, and given a real insight into everyday life Up North that really is not on the tourist route.

Over the years the Americans reciprocated; indeed the Friendship Force is global and still going to this day. Not a bad idea for a President. When the Friendship Force hit its 10th anniversary we were sent on a three-week jolly to the States to shoot a documentary on the whole thing.

It included interviews with Jimmy and his lovely wife Rosalynn. A few days before our holiday – maybe holiday isn't the right word – there was a big problem with our work visas and travel documents.

When you visit certain countries around the world you need what is called a carnet, a passport for the camera and kit to show you actually own it and have not just bought the gear abroad and saved the import tax on the stuff. You have to have one and it has to be in order, with all the corresponding serial numbers on the carnet that match the ones on the kit.

It's a great game, and the American authorities play it very well. I know of several flights been missed because some big hairy-arsed immigration guy has one digit too many on one of the half dozen batteries that are laid out in front of him, so they go through the whole kit, and that can take hours. It's a bit like bingo really, but without the laughs.

Anyway, Jimmy was informed that his favourite British TV crew was having a bit of stress coming over to see him, so the next day our producer popped down to the American Embassy in London, and what do you know, all sorted. In fact I think we were made citizens, (not quite) but our work visas pretty much guaranteed that we could work in the States wherever and whenever we liked. If Jimmy were ever to start up a tourist company, buy shares in it! It would be stress-free travelling.

We were to fly across the pond via Schiphol, Holland's main international airport, but to get there we had to take a shuttle flight from Newcastle Airport. I have never been able to work out when a late night becomes an early morning.

At 4am we checked our kit in via Holland to be picked up in Atlanta USA. In other words, goodbye kit. Never ever ever put anything valuable or anything you might need in the hold of an aircraft. A good rule of thumb here is never put anything in the hold of an aircraft and expect to pick it up on the other side of the world.

Now the camera and all the main kit we use always comes along with us in the cabin. Yes, there'll be rows with cabin crew, but once you're on board and holding up the flight, they always find room for the kit, no matter how full they say they are. It's a sort of game – give them the cost of the camera, lens and microphones and they soon sympathise with you. The down side is, you just don't seem to get that much free booze, as you have just become a problem passenger.

No sooner had we taken off and got up a few thousand feet than we started descending. Schiphol by air from Newcastle or Teesside takes about 35 minutes and now we were falling like a stone after ten minutes.

"Is there a problem?" I enquired.

"No, Sir, no problem. We're just landing at Teesside to pick up our passengers there as we do every morning, " I was told.

We had got up early and driven an hour and a half to Newcastle to catch a flight back down to where we had just left. Great.

As we flew over my house into the airport that's at the end of my drive, the producer who'd booked the travel arrangements got a right fucking ear full, I can tell you. Sorry wasn't good enough. He knew we'd make him pay for this.

Everything else went according to plan though. After we did some filming in the cockpit of the KLM 747 whilst crossing the pond, we'd noticed that first class looked extremely empty, and it seemed a real shame not to use it, so we did. Nobody seemed to mind and when we explained that Jimmy Carter would be well impressed that KLM had looked after his favourite TV crew for him, nothing seemed to be a problem. After vast amounts of booze, the crew promised to look into having a dartboard put up for the return journey.

"Everyone knew that Jimmy flies with a dartboard!"

We really were pushing it. Our hosts in Atlanta were a lovely couple called Jonny and Gerry Johnson. Nothing was too much trouble for them. In fact Les has been over to the States many times to see them and they too have been to the UK on numerous occasions. In fact, they helped arrange the wedding of my stepsister Lisa and her boyfriend Ian, who, when visiting one time with Les and his wife Sybs, decided on the spur of the moment to get married. It looked a fabulous location judging by the photos.

Jonny was a WW11 pilot who went on to fly for many years with Eastern Airlines and met Gerry in the air when she worked as a senior stewardess. One afternoon I'll never forget is when Jonny got all his WW11 flying mates round for a bit of a session – as they say, drinking mash and talking trash, or is it the other way round? The stories were just unbelievable and I sat there all afternoon just open-mouthed.

The filming was going well. We met a lot of those first folk that flew over with Carter and recorded their memories about who they met and where they'd been. Quite a bit of the material for the documentary had already been shot ten years earlier when TV crews followed them around for several days in the UK, so not really that much effort was needed.

In fact Jonny stuck us all in his big RV and we took off down to Florida for a few days of R and R, chilling out on Daytona Beach, drinking Bud, and taking in the sights. At this point I would once again like to thank the BBC licence payer – 5 star dining, top class hotels and bubbly is not cheap, but it was all part of the programme-making process, and the documentary would not have been half as good if we hadn't eaten fillet steak, lobster and caviar every night. The fine wines were a necessity.

After our very arduous schedule, all that was left to do was an interview with Mr and Mrs Carter and that was it. Jimmy Carter has a peanut ranch in deepest Georgia. It's also a tourist attraction and even has an exact replica of the Oval room found in the White House.

He had not long been out of office and security was tight, even for his British boys. We were doing the interviews with them in the Oval room. It was a big interview for me, and I checked and double-checked all my equipment. I knew I couldn't fuck this one up. Besides that, I'd never met an ex-President before and I hoped things would go smoothly. They did to start with. Jimmy was lovely. He put us all at ease and really did have a soft spot for the North East, its people and everything connected to it. It made us quite proud.

He remembered every little detail about his visit some ten years earlier and he told us one or two stories off the record. One night he disappeared with his host down the pub, having given 30 or so special agents the slip, to have a bottle of Brown with the locals. As he walked in the pub the lads just looked up, wished him well and carried on drinking, with one or two asking his thoughts about the weather. Can you imagine the scenario? I believe one or two senior heads rolled after that event.

"Call the White House. The President is missing. No! Cancel that, he's down the boozer with the lads!" or so the story goes!

I was listening to the audio coming though my headphones making sure the needles didn't hit the red and distort the sound, and listening for any loud background noise – planes, birds, lawnmowers, that sort of thing.

The interviewer was our local well-known presenter Mike Neville, a great guy and a true professional. The interview was going brilliantly well and we were on the last question, when I heard a loud squeak coming from a door across the room. With that a head popped around. I gave her my fuck off stare and she just stared back. The bloody woman was screwing up the most important interview of my life.

If she lent on that door anymore I would have had to stop the interview and go over and punch her! I mouthed fuck off to her and she disappeared. She had learnt her lesson well and closed the door so slowly it didn't squeak closed. Within seconds, a head popped round a second door. It was the same face, the same woman ruining my sound. The secret service guys sitting round the room looked at her and then looked at me.

Mike and Jimmy were oblivious to what was going on. She was making the door squeak and I was about to ask one of the guys to just shoot her, before I blew my top.

As she left for the second time I again mouthed fuck off and pointed with my arm, just get out and never come back. She was having a laugh. She appeared back at the first squeaky door. I was boiling. The sound this time was unusable from the door noise so I mouthed a really big fuck off at the very same time Mike had finished the interview. I took the neck mic off Jimmy and he asked if everything had been OK.

"Yes!" I replied as this bloody woman came walking towards us to explain herself.

"This had better be good!" I thought as she got nearer. "She'd better be telling him about a nuclear war that was about to start, or something equally important."

She was now at Carter's side. Jimmy turned to us and said: "This is my lovely wife, Rosalynn. I believe you're interviewing her next!"

TOP THAT! I died. Please God take me now. Let the ground swallow me up and I'll quite happily spend the rest of eternity in a pit of fire. What have I just said, and to whom?

Surely I could be put to death for that? The worst thing was she apologised for making a noise when she entered. Please don't rub my nose in it any more, I thought.

The interview seemed to go on for ages; at no point did I get eye contact with her. I thought about crying and then just killing myself. What the hell did the secret service guys think? God knows.

Here they are, guarding these people, and I'm sitting in their living room, telling her to fuck off and looking to kill her! If one had been about to just pop me there and then, it would have been a blessing.

The documentary went out to great reviews. The trip had been great and the people lovely. The States do get a bad press but all the people I've ever met from there have been wonderful, and I really love the place.

This story has been told by numerous people over the years and, needless to say, embellished. The documentary went out with the title of "All the President's Friends"… except one!

Das Boot / The ARK

One day Les arrived home with a speed boat, as you do. This guy he knew wanted a promotional video doing on his boat-building company and, as payment, gave Les a speed boat. It seemed like a good idea at the time.

It then needed equipping with little things like the engine and such like; not to mention water skis, wet suits, in fact everything. It then had to be registered and permits got before we could use it on Ullswater in the Lake District, my favourite Cumbrian lake.

The only thing we didn't have was any advice or instructions on how to water ski, but hey how hard could that be? After many weeks or was it years, we finally cracked it and my brother and I both became quite good, even getting to the stage of monoski-ing.

After many wonderful weekends in one of the most beautiful parts of the world, we were hoyed off the Lake after the bloody authorities imposed a speed limit, so we had to decamp and use Windermere with its many restrictions and wardens worse than traffic cops. We were forever being bollocked for ski-ing and speeding in the wrong place, even in November with snow falling, and below freezing, and with not a soul on the 22-mile lake except for us. The Trotski bastards still managed to find us and threaten us with deportation to the colonies for some minor speeding offence.

Les had worked out it was probably cheaper to buy another boat to sleep on than spending a fortune on B&Bs and eating out, so with much encouragement from us, he went out and bought a beautiful cruiser called Alma 11. She could sleep four very comfortably but eleven at a push. She was the ultimate gin palace despite being moored in the wrong part of the world.

Party time was now in the Lake District, and over the years all sorts of shit happened but no one actually ever went to jail. One or two got arrested now and then. We used to moor her up in a beautiful little harbour and jump into the speed boat and get pissed up in the numerous bars and hotels that lined the lake's shores, and then play a great game of finding Alma in the dark.

I am pretty sure there were no lights on the speed boat, and yes, for sure we would be hoyed off the Lake if caught by the warden travelling flat out in the dark, pissed up and reckless, laughing and screaming over the noise of the engine every time we went out. It was very, very irresponsible indeed – very dangerous, but seriously exhilarating. No one ever worked out if there was a drink drive rule on the water. I guess because no one ever asked!

One night getting very pissed in Windermere Marina, it all got a bit out of hand. Alma was alone in the dark somewhere on the Lake. I seem to remember it being Jonny's (my brother's) birthday because someone, maybe Baz, had just thrown him off a balcony and into the Marina swimming pool. Needless to say, we were asked to leave and I believe we were barred, which was quite common.

We staggered out of the complex and made for the jetty where I think I left the small boat. The Marina there was quite large and we just used to moor up wherever there was space, mostly in someone else's paid-for space. The small lights that illuminate the jetties are as good as useless, but after a while I managed to find the place where I thought I'd left it.

But walking up to the spot it was plainly obvious it wasn't there – gone, stolen, call the Police. We all agreed that it was definitely the area where we had come ashore some hours earlier, but now there was no boat. How were we going to get back to the other one?

What would Les say when we told him we'd lost his pride and joy? Right, in a situation like this there is only one thing to do, find a boozer and get wasted. All agreed. As we all staggered about scratching our heads, Baz shouts up "I found it!"

Thank Hell for that, I thought!

Baz carried on: "It's sort of where you left it, but not in the same place."

He pointed, and we all looked down his arm to his finger and beyond that and into the water, where you could just make out the outline of the speedboat neatly settled at the bottom of the marina!

In the morning the marina people used a big crane and brought it back onto dry land, much to the amusement of the many happy sailors, who were getting stuck in to breakfast, and trying to work out which arseholes owned a small wet speed boat.

The problem was that there was a small bung at the stern of the boat and it wasn't in. Come to think of it the bilge pump had been working overtime that day so we hadn't noticed it, and when you're flying along, not much water would get in anyway.

The boat would and did dry out. It wasn't so much a problem with the plastic and leather, but the electrics and the engine were another thing. Even back then the engine cost somewhere in the region of around three grand.

So with lashings of WD40 and a quick prayer and a turn of the key! Bingo! It was working, the old man would never know. I did regale the story to him some 20 years later at my brother's wedding.

Well, most if it. A shrug of the shoulders is all I got. How can you be pissed off with something that happened so long ago? Anyway worse things happen at sea!

Still on the subject of the sea, being a Piscean, I love the water, sea, lakes, rivers, all aspects of the wet stuff. Even more so I love boats and ships, and on many occasions I have filmed the launching of war ships, mainly Type 42 Destroyers. In fact anything that was launched on the Tyne at Swan Hunters ship yard I would always ask to cover.

I can even remember the last ship to be launched on the River Tees. To see these majestic beasts rolling down a slipway and into the river makes the hair on the back of my neck stand up. It's just amazing.

In fact a few years ago we did one being launched into the Clyde, and I got the same sense of awe and marvel as I did the first time I saw one go down. In Newcastle even the local schools used to close so everyone could witness these events. But the most important people there were the lads, skilled craftsmen, turners, fitters, welders, joiners, chippies and everyone associated with the ship, who were all there to witness these spectacles. These people were the life and soul of the river, and generations of shipbuilders worked in the yards – sons, fathers, and grandfathers all took great pride in what they did and always built a great product. It's all gone tits up now, and the skills of the men that made ships on the Tyne, Tees and Wear are in the process of being lost if they haven't already been lost.

With thousands of good men having lost their jobs year after year, there's no one left to build ships anymore. It really does make my heart bleed. We still need ships, and for whatever reason they're not being built up here. With the loss of every job a family is plunged into crisis. Repeat that many thousands of times over, and you get problems. What is there for the lads to do? It's very sad.

Anyway I digress, we were sent out to do the sea trials of HMS ARK Royal, the pride of the British Naval fleet, and a fantastic aircraft carrier. The statistics about her are mind-blowing. We were flying out to meet her from Newcastle Airport on a Navy Sea King chopper, but at the last minute the weather had got very bad. It had been bad for a few days but now it was blowing a force 9, so that job was up the spout then.

But as we were leaving the Airport the Naval PR people told us that there would be a small weather window of a few hours, which meant we might be able to fly out to her, do a few laps round the North Sea and get back before it was definitely too dangerous.

The Ark was at anchor just a few miles off Tynemouth, so with my prayer book in one hand and my worry beads in the other, we took off for a very enjoyable flight out to her. The wind had dropped to a very calm 7 or 8, and at one point I really did start to think that maybe I was a tad too young to die, but the PR people had a show to put on, so death would just have to wait.

We landed on her in what I can only describe as tumble dryer conditions. This mighty vessel was bobbing about like a tiny little cork. Landing a helicopter in conditions like this is very dangerous, if the pilot gets it wrong and drops onto the deck as she is coming up you get what I think is called a hard landing, (a crash!). The consequences just don't bear thinking about, so I didn't. In fact with your eyes tightly shut it's really not too bad at all. The pilots were the best in the world, so you've got a good starters for ten.

We landed and were promptly ushered down into the bowels of the ship for a briefing and a buffet reception of vol au vents and curried eggs.

Now in my defence it had to be said the night before was a big one and I could still feel the curry and lager swilling around in my stomach and after the flight things were starting to take their toll. I have never been sick at sea or in the air.

Normally it doesn't bother me, even on a small prawn boat in a gale force 7, I still remained well even through you physically couldn't stand up for hours due to the conditions. One minute there was sky and the next time you looked up there were waves, but this time things were different.

I had hot and cold flushes, and went from white to red and then to a somewhat green colour. To all and sundry it looked like I was doing a very good chameleon impersonation, and banging through the vast waves on the North Sea at full pelt wasn't helping at all. I felt like I had bird flu, swine flu and E-Coli all at the same time.

For the first time in my life I felt punch drunk and it wasn't long before my legs just buckled, and down I went like the proverbial sack of spuds. The Navy personnel all looked on with sympathy and smiles, but looking round at the rest of the media pack I knew there were a few not far behind me.

Off I was carted to the sick bay – the first person ever to be taken into the medical area suffering, not from the spoils of war, but bloody seasickness. The place was all brand new with covers and wrappers on all the hi-tech equipment. They had all that was needed to cope with any medical emergencies.

Some kind Navy guy gave me a load of tablets and a bucket, put me on a bed and let me get on with it. Even before he had left the room, the contents of my stomach were swilling around in a brand new yellow medical bucket.

He smiled, turned around and said: "Congratulations, son. You're the first one to christen the medical bay."

I felt an utter twat. The lads were seriously going to have my life on this one. Embarrassment just wasn't the word.

After a few laps up and down the sea it was time to leave. Never before have I been as pleased to see a chopper in my life as the one that took me off that ship, despite the horrendous flying conditions.

I would rather take my chances in the air than spend another second on board. I was of course ridiculed over the incident and several decades on still am by those that were there.

But what a claim to fame. I was the first person ever to be admitted to the sick bay on the brand new HMS ARK ROYAL. To this day I have never been sick at sea, but have the greatest sympathy for anyone who suffers from seasickness …ha.

The Miners' Strike

I have covered riots and civil unrest many times over the years. As a matter of course I carry a hard hat and stab vest in the truck; in fact only this weekend I was wearing them covering the English Defence League and their chums, the Anti Fascist League. But nothing has, and I suspect ever will, scare the living shit out of me like the Miners' Strike.

The race riots of Oldham and Bradford were interesting, and when the Meadow Well estate went up, along with most of the West End of Newcastle, it certainly got the pulse racing, with bricks coming in through the car windows and people on my bonnet with crow bars and baseball bats trying to kill me. It does make you wonder if you've chosen the right profession, but the Miners' Strike was, to me, one long year of pure violence – just what a 17-year-old trainee needs in his first year of work.

1984. I remember it well, having crashed out of 6th form due to extreme boredom and not understanding any of the course work, it was time for a proper job. I was all for buying an ice cream van and making millions down in Cornwall with a mate, until someone asked what I was going to do during the winter months.

So while I was plotting world domination in the ice cream business, I was told to pick up Les's tripod and do a bit of telly until something more interesting came along. Les was running a three-man crew – himself the cameraman, Steve Luck, his sound recordist and me gofer.

I learnt a lot and quickly. First never say no, and second always get your round in. There. I was qualified. I was also given a good bit of advice when I first started. Get a good pension scheme and buy the warmest, most waterproof jacket on the market.

Up North at night in winter you will need it, they told me.

Also technology had just changed. On Friday Les was shooting on film and the sound recordist was using a Nargra, and on Monday he was shooting video on tape. It doesn't sound much now, but it revolutionized the industry.

There were still some drawbacks with the gear; one being the weight of the recorder, and the fact that you had to have an umbilical cord between camera and recorder. Putting a tape straight into the camera was some years off.

So the first few months of this new technology, everyone was wrapping each other round lampposts and letterboxes, and tearing the connections out at either end. It made running fun, you really did have to think as one. Cameramen being cameramen just fucking take off. It wasn't long before I was using this new video stuff myself and Les's three-man crew became a two-man crew, him and me.

Even now some quarter of a century after the strike, in certain pit villages amongst certain families and communities there is still hatred and resentment between those that striked and those that went back to work. It affected everyone in those villages and it took its toll. The strike also took its toll on a few coppers and media alike. You've seen the pictures of horses charging, bricks flying, batons waving. The miners really were fighting for their jobs, and sometimes their lives as well.

However history may look back at what happened, Scargill was right believing lose the strike and lose the pits. Thatcher broke it. It was a war she could not dare to lose.

Over the years I have watched the decline of the coal industry in and around the Durham coalfields, and North East generally, yet we still need coal. The mines have gone, the seams not worked and the pits flooded. Thousands were flung onto the dole queues, communities and pit villages went into a massive decline with no hope, no jobs and, for many living there, no future. It's very sad to see.

I can still remember being present as the last pit ponies were brought out of the mines and put out to grass. Now it's all gone. The odd pit head and winding gear still remains here and there as a testament to the last great Northern industry. Ironic really but on some of the pit land, employment centres and job clubs have set up to try to retrain the lads, but believe you me there are no proper jobs (see Billy Elliot and The Full Monty).

These lads weren't made to be computer programmers or production line workers. They were miners just like their fathers and before them their grandfathers. I've been taking those sorts of shots that appear in those movies for years. The atmosphere in Seaham, Horden, Easington and many other places to me remains the same.

My memories of the strike will stick with me for life – the broken bones, the blood, unconscious men being trampled by horses. The noise, the charges on both sides, the sheer aggression on people's faces, the hatred. The police were Thatcher's boys. They were the enemy and beatings were given out on both sides, and the media were stuck in the middle.

No one wanted us there but it was our job to be there, and it wasn't long before we too become a priory target. If you were sent to cover a certain pit and you were the only ones there taking pictures and the pictures appeared on the nightly news and the police came in and looked at the material and the protesters were subsequently arrested, then it doesn't take much working out that if you remove the cameraman then no photos could be taken and no evidence gathered.

I remember one morning at Easington pit, there were a dozen or so lads with balaclavas and baseball bats waiting for us, just for us, the BBC crew. We were singled out for special treatment and we got it. Steve Luck had a lump of concrete thrown at him hitting him on his back, and that was his career over. Almost disabled, he just couldn't carry the gear any more and needed quite a lot of treatment and left the industry.

The following day, without taking an exam, or come to think of it, even having an interview, I was promoted to sound recordist first class, and promised an extra shiny sixpence in my pay packet.

I did indeed have sleepless nights and cold sweats, and wondered what the fuck I'd let myself in for. Some job eh? I should have stuck to plan A and sold ice cream. The weeks and months passed but there was always the underlying violence waiting to rear its ugly head.

I remember another time when several hundred miners broke into a car park inside the colliery grounds, and you have to remember that these were big burly lads, used to hard work, and who enjoyed a good scrap. They proceeded to pick up cars and throw them through the windows; thirty or so lads picking up a car at a time and fucking propelling it through the air and into windows. This wasn't some film set action. This was for real, and this sort of fun continued for most of the year.

One day the boss (lovely bloke by the name of John Bird) had a great idea. He wanted us to be on the picket line to see the scabs being escorted in to work. That's when the fun starts, and repeats itself when they leave, but get this! He then wanted us to get onto one of the battle buses with some scabs, cross the picket line with them, and then follow them down the pit, to do a bit of a Day in the Life of.

As great ideas go, it was a pearler! So we did. We tried to point out that fuck all goes on down the pit as 99% of the miners are above ground standing on the picket line, but it fell on deaf ears.

Didn't we just have a great day? The bus was duly bricked, but lying on the floor covered in coats and jackets so as not to be recognised, we only heard the thuds. Well, not really thuds, more like bolts of lightning, not very frightening at all!

Going down the pit and travelling five miles out under the North Sea to see fuck all, was almost as much fun as the bus ride in. Still we got the pics and as the Beeb was almost completely controlled by Thatcher, they were used for her political ends.

I did see coppers linking arms and holding their pay cheques up to the strikers and baiting them. A lot of lads made a lot of money in overtime. One cameraman I knew had a massive extension put on his house and called it Scargill Tower.

One day we turned up on the picket line and some burly-arsed miners knew our names. That was most disconcerting; in fact very worrying. It turned out they were from the Easington Allotment Club and as it happened we were shooting that weekend a programme for the local BBC – a show called, funnily enough, The Allotment Show, which was massive with growers up North.

The producer had given them our names. All hell was kicking off, bricks were flying, horses were charging, people were screaming and bleeding and these lads wanted us to know that their allotments weren't in as pristine condition as they should be due to an outbreak of potato scab. Now you just couldn't make that up.

Still it was good to have them on board, even for a few hours. We pulled out all the stops at the weekend for that show, I can tell you! Never have allotments looked so good, even with an outbreak of potato scab!

But funny moments were few and far between and I quit my job at least a dozen times that year and was glad when it was all over; glad but sad. These lads now had nothing, and had truly suffered and now their pits had closed and there was no work.

Their memories will never fade. Still to this day father won't talk to son because of their beliefs. The saying "like taking coals to Newcastle" does not now apply due cheap imports. And still no one has learnt anything.

So now when I cover a few pissed-off hippies, or right wing boneheads pushing the police, or the occasional riot that lasts a day or two, I hark back to the good old days when I was terrified shitless every day for a whole year!

The death of Margaret Thatcher did not come as a great surprise to me, she was after all an old and frail lady. I have over the years filmed her many times, and its nice to see again the pictures we took of her at the Metro Centre in Gateshead, and her walk in the wilderness here on Teesside. I'd go as far as to say they were iconic pictures of her. I'm sitting on the fence a bit here (most unlike me), but my views about her and her policies have changed somewhat over the years, so I'm going to leave it at this and just say, whatever you may think about her, we can all agree... she knew how to draw a crowd.

Gemma

I am a "dog-killing bastard". To this day I still deny this alarming claim, as made by my wife. Technically I did not actually take the life of the quietest, most loving, caring little West Highland Terrier on the planet, but I may as well have done.

Gemma, was Julia's dog, and she got her as a pup. In fact, she had two, Zoe being the other one, but she was the most vicious little bastard you had ever come across and was put down for biting people.

Gemma, however, was completely different. At 13 years old, she was getting on a bit, dribbling and snapping at the boys who were just toddlers, so we knew that her time was short. The dog was loved by everyone except Baz. For some reason she hated men with beards. Tashes were ok, but not beards, and indeed the dog had a great life.

When we were busy Jue's parents or one of our friends had her. She was never a problem to anyone. One day I announced that we were going on holiday, somewhere down the Med. It was all booked, so grab your trunks, here comes the sun.

A few days later Julia announced that we couldn't go on holiday, as there was no one to look after the dog. Jue's parents were away, and friends were all away or busy, we were stuck with the dog! Bollock that, I said, it's going into kennels and we are going on holiday. But Gemma, the world's most spoilt pooch, had never even seen a kennel, let alone stayed in one.

The holiday came around, and I got my way. We headed for the sun and she headed for the kennels. The flight times meant that if there were no delays on the way back I could just make kick off to watch the Boro play Man U, and amazingly I did. Man U tortured us again, but we did score, so better than last time.

I had a few beers with the lads after the game and went home, only to find Jue sitting on the back door step crying her eyes out and snotting into a hanky.

"Don't worry, love, it's only a game and we never get anything off Man U anyway, " I quipped.

She turned and looked me straight in the eye.

"You killed her! Gemma is dead!"

Oh shit! Crying on my shoulder, she launched into the details as told to her by the kennel owner, who somewhat embellished the story, bastard. Apparently, Gemma could not settle and pined and pined, and thinking she had been abandoned, she wouldn't eat. After three unsettling days she just gave up and was found dead one morning.

The kennel owner bastard had gone into great detail about how the very loved little dog had just given up the cause; in fact he finished by saying he was sure that Gemma died of a broken heart.

"A broken heart, the bastard! Could he not have just said she passed away peacefully of old age?" I asked.

It was all my fault anyhow, and I have had to carry the can for it ever since! Not only that, he wanted the full week's board for her and a shedload more to boot, as he had had to pay the vet for disposing of her body, so the moral of the story is – don't get a dog, they cost a packet and die on you, simples.

Raquel Welch

Talking of beautiful babes, many people of my generation will remember that iconic pose struck by Raquel Welch for the film 10, 000 years BC. She was at one stage one of the world's best known and most gorgeous Hollywood actresses, so when she was up North and spending a few days on my patch I was all ears.

Her son was about to marry Fred Trueman's daughter, or was it the other way round? Who cares? She was going to be staying in a hotel down the road and it was my job to get some pictures of this Hollywood icon. How her son and Trueman's daughter got it together in the first place is anyone's guess, but they were getting married in a small church in North Yorkshire and indeed the circus came to town.

Fred Trueman was a true Yorkshireman right down to his toe nails. He was an ex England cricket legend, and bristled with every Yorkshire trait possible, right down to his no-nonsense crap about anything, including, we believe, his stance to major, A-list Hollywood actors.

The first meeting between the two sets of prospective parents sharing black pudding and pie and peas must have been a sight to behold. What could they have possibly talked about or indeed have in common? I guess we'll never know but the media pack sure had its own ideas.

It was one of those jobs that I enjoyed from start to finish, and the stories and memories about the whole event became more and more unbelievable, especially from the American and European papara-tizzi that had descended to cover the event.

I was put up in the same hotel as Raquel's party, a seriously nice place called the Devonshire Arms, in a quintessential North Yorkshire hamlet of Bolton Abbey, picture postcard stuff, with the Duke of Devonshire pretty much owning most things round about.

The hotel, needless to say, didn't want any of those low life media scum on its premises and put the room rates up accordingly. I managed to get a room, no budget for this one – the pics were going globally and price was not an issue and if my room was five or six doors away from hers then so much the better.

If I had to slum it in the Devonshire suite and eat in the renowned restaurants, and stay four nights drinking fine wine, then I would just have to grin and bear it. Someone had to do it, and why not me?

In return I just had to get some exclusive footage that could be hawked around the world agencies. No problem, or so I thought.

I arrived the same day as Miss Welch's party on the Wednesday and the wedding was on the Saturday, so I had plenty of time. She was with her partner at the time – Bungalow Bill. Read into that what you want, but all the "upstairs" jokes were strictly taboo.

The hotel was pissed off I was staying, but having paid up front for three days, there was not much they could do. The public bars were swamped with hacks and snappers 24/7 and the waiters, chefs, bar tenders and groundsmen were being bunged wads of cash for any tittle tattle that they heard or saw.

I'm afraid that's just the way it works, and it works very well. I saw one barman being given at least two weeks' wages in cash for a few lines of copy. What goes around comes around, I, on the other hand, worked and still do strictly above board. In fact, all TV news media do, but papers were and still are a law unto themselves. But gossip sells papers and we buy them, so don't criticise it too much; otherwise you'd have nothing to read in the morning with your Frosties.

The hotel did its best to keep the paps at bay by closing off the restaurant for them, telling everyone they were out, pulling tractors and grass cutters across roads and car parks whenever they left or returned, lots of great tricks that are still used today by those stars that don't want to have their magazine and TV documentaries ruined by the media, but who still go crawling to them when they fall on hard times.

I was flapping a bit by now after three days living it up on exes and I'd not seen sight nor sound of Raquel. London was giving me some stress. What was I suppose to do, knock on her door and ask for a chat? Well frankly yes. I had already chipped in with the lads for a big bouquet of flowers for her in the hope of a picture, but sadly to no avail.

We did get a nice hand-written reply telling us to fuck off. Actually it read: "You are not the paparazzi and I am not your diva."

Some of the less well-educated media wanted to know why she was referring to her herself as some type of car, until their little error was pointed out, but still no one was having any joy.

That is until the Friday night before the wedding and joy it certainly was. Raquel and party were definitely in the hotel. They had been seen and were moping around the hotel talking to their PR people. I was on sentry duty, doing recon in the hotel bar where I had been doing a lot of recon, and getting nothing except a bad head.

It was late, very late and I was loath to leave my post, but under duress I did and took off with a small hunting party, not quite sure what we were going to achieve. The couple of lads I was with were paps that had flown in from the States and were going to get a picture whatever the cost.

I, on the other hand, had a video camera and needed at least a ten second shot of her, but where was she? She was in fact by this time back in her room, and these two nutters were all for diving in, banging off a few frames and then legging it. I tried to explain that wasn't how we operated in the UK, but it fell on deaf ears. Even when I pointed out it was illegal and we'd get arrested, lose our jobs and go to jail, they still didn't seem to care. But now it was all too late. We were standing outside her room (her son and future daughter-in-law were staying at Fred's pad and only visited the hotel a few times).

One of the lads looked through the key hole and the other tried to look under the door. We were whispering as quietly as church mice. It was not a good situation to be caught in and I told them I'd see them back at the bar, with a clear conscience. As I turned to leave one hissed and beckoned me close to the door.

"They're on the job!" he mouthed to me.

Oh fuck, surely a little listen isn't going to send me down, I thought. So I put my ear to the door. Sure enough Bungalow Bill and Raquel Welch were at it. They were making sweet love and I was listening. That's it – I'm off, I thought. Okay, one more thrust and I'm off. No, I'm definitely off. God, if I got caught, listing to this…Oh shit, she's coming; they're coming together! Oh just leave Karl!

I ran back to the safety of the bar and ordered a nerve-quenching Stella, trying to imagine the bedroom scenario.

The wedding went as planned. The bride and groom were already at the altar when she turned up very late in an open-topped carriage wearing, well truthfully, not very much. She had on a very tight black curve-hugging short dress, that left nothing to the imagination – great for a night club, not so sure for a wedding though.

I suspect words might have been said, but then what humble bride can out-do a genuine real-life diva? Can you imagine Fred's face, daughter at the altar with her bridegroom, waiting for the mother-in-law? But that's Hollywood!

As for me, four days on the lash, thousands spent and not a single shot till she got to the church. But hey, out of all the people there I was one of the few that knew what she got up to the night before the wedding. Your secret's been safe with me Raquel, until now!

Dirty Harry

In my view all guns should be banned, and that includes air guns and crossbows. There's never a year goes by when some kid somewhere gets a pellet lodged in an eye socket, or worse.

Hunting and shooting accidents happen all the time when guns are around. I'm not a killjoy but the risks far outweigh the pros. I am unsure about Olympic shooting sports or the lads that bang away on the grouse moors, but thank God we're not like the States and their constitution, about having the right to bear arms.

Even in our own Isles if guns were banned and outlawed and made almost impossible to get hold of, then maybe Dunblane might never have happened. Who knows?

It's quite common unfortunately to see coppers carrying machine guns in our cities and airports and at big court cases, but good not to see everyday Bobby carrying one!

VIPS, royals and senior politicians all have protection officers that have firearms, and unfortunately that's just the way it is, even one of Blair's boys once discharged his firearm on a train that Blair was on.

We once did a story about just how easy it is to get a gun, and I was asked if I could get hold of one; needless to say it was going to be handed straight in to the police. After half a day I was able, via several phone calls, to get hold of a shotgun with several rounds, serial number removed. I never saw the gun or indeed bought it, but I was then asked to get hold of something a bit sexier, like an Uzi.

A few days later and a bit of pump money and I was assured I could get one from Liverpool area. The shotgun would have cost about £120 but the Uzi was about £1500, and that was with a few hundred rounds. My bottle went and I wanted no more to do with getting hold of sub machine guns. Imagine being caught with one of them. They'd just lock you up and throw away the key, even if I was on my way to hand it in. There would have been some explaining to do. It just simply wasn't worth the risk, or indeed the mandatory five years in clink.

I passed the info onto the relevant people and left it at that. Frightening to think those things are on our streets, and it's left up to the police and us in the media to try and make sense what happened after an incident.

I was involved in an incident with a handgun that nearly cost a man his life. It still haunts me. We were doing a job at a gun club. We had got pics of people firing different weapons at targets, in a very controlled environment. After we had finished the bloke in charge asked if we'd like a go.

"Yeah sure, why not!" I said.

After a quick briefing he passed me a set of ear protectors and a Magnum 45, the gun was used by Clint Eastwood in the Dirty Harry films. He filled it full of bullets and, keeping the barrel pointing away from him, passed it to me and told me to aim at the large targets.

On films you see arms going in the air after the gun is first fired – well, that's how it is. The recoil sends your arms flying up and if you're not standing properly, it will have you on your arse. It's unbelievably powerful, but as I found out, especially for a first timer like me, it's impossible to hit anything, I would have missed a barn door at two feet.

Accidents and incidents happen in milliseconds. You always have to be on your game when you have a gun, and I wasn't. After about three rounds and thinking it was impossible to hit anything with it, it jammed.

I turned to the instructor still pushing down on the trigger to explain this to him. Like lighting he kicked it out of my hands. It was not till I got back to the car did I go white and nearly pass out.

The whole episode was over in the blink of an eye, but not being used to guns and having one jam on you, I just wanted the guy to fix it. I was pointing it straight at his chest and pushing on the trigger of one of the most powerful handguns in the world.

The bloke wasn't pleased. His gun was muddy and he nearly died. I'm not sure who was shaking the most. We didn't say a word. I haven't touched a gun since that incident. They're too dangerous, and I don't trust myself with them.

Colonel Spooner's Tie

The Royal Signals' motorcycle display team is well loved and well known. Based at Catterick Garrison, they put on death-defying shows for the pleasure of thousands all over the world, as well as helping the Army out on the PR front.

The lads themselves are a great bunch, but take it from me, they are also barking mad. In Army talk we were "tasked" to follow them for a whole year, on and off the field, so to speak, culminating in the Allied Forces' day parade in Berlin.

I still maintain it was one of the very first Doc-u-soaps put out on air. With literally hundreds of hours shot, the series went out on BBC 2, with great reviews.

It all starts with a selection process, and those who avoid broken arms, legs, ribs, and not going under the surgeon's knife in their efforts to get in are rewarded with a two-year drinking and shagging pass, on the proviso that they sometimes have to get on the occasional bike and do a few tricks.

All these young eager lads line up and get given a high-powered motorcycle and are told to ride up 1in1 hills until they either get good at it or die. Most have never ridden a bike before and that first morning watching them crash into each other and any unmoveable object made an outtake Christmas tape all of their own.

Over the following days, weeks and months we watched and

recorded the process of turning these normal squaddies into individual Evil Kenevils – fearless, brave, some may even say daft.

But once you were in, it was basically two years on the piss, interrupted by the occasional show. The perks were great, and so was the travel, and to be fair it was a good gig. The accidents were horrendous, with some stuff simply too graphic to show.

After they had progressed and learnt the moves on smaller trails bikes, they were then given their show bikes – 750 Triumphs, a very fast powerful bike that can do a lot of damage.

The guy in charge was Colonel Spooner, who loved the fact that the Beeb was going to show the Army in a good light. He had this theory the film would up the recruiting process, and so we got complete access and some great footage.

But the real guy in charge was Sergeant Gary Ellerson, who is still a good family friend to this day, so without telling tales out of school I will miss out all the stuff about heavy drinking sessions and regular trips down Berlin's red light district, as I may well also incriminate myself too.

Things went swimmingly well and the year passed all too quickly. We got a real insight into Army life and met some great guys. The life was good, but the discipline did my head in. I have never been one for discipline or authority – too many wankers in too many high positions, but I accept in the forces it just has to be. Under fire with your life literally at times in your colleagues' hands, you have to know that you can depend on them and that's when all the training and the shit you have put up with comes into play. We see it all too often on our TVs.

Anyway we were flying out to Berlin to meet up with the lads and follow them through the Allied Forces' day parade, the highlight of the year. Communism was in full swing and the fall of the wall was yet to happen. There were strict rules relating to travel in and out of Berlin, which meant flying into one of Berlin's airports at under 3, 000 feet. Don't ask me why.

For two hours we went through the worst thunderstorm I have ever experienced. On a military flight the highest ranking officer on board is pointed out. I expect that is because if the bar service runs out, you need someone to complain to. But I am sure I saw him praying. I, on the other hand, had just given up the will to live. Surely death won't be as frightening as this, and as we landed, I stopped crying.

We had several days before the big event and saw some sights. We even did some sight-seeing. Crossing through Checkpoint Charlie and going into East Berlin still under Soviet Rule was all very strange. It was my first time in a communist country. There were bread queues and those Lada-type cars called Trabants. Bomber Harris certainly did a job on it, as did the Russians and the loss of life on both sides is mind blowing.

We were, as befits any TV crew, staying in the officers' mess, basically a 5 star hotel. They know what side their bread's buttered on. I don't know were the grunts were staying, but I'm sure the Chablis wasn't as brutally chilled as ours was!

One night we decided to eat in the officers' mess with the officers, but a big shock to me was you had to dress for dinner and wear a tie, bit of an arse really. No jeans or T-Shirts were allowed, which is, of course, the standard dress for most crews. I managed to scrounge everything – trousers, shirt but no tie. In fact at one point three of us were going to have to share one. We pointed this small fact out to Colonel Spooner, who we were dining with.

All the tie shops were shut. It was late, and we were snookered. No one thought to bring a tie, so how high would they hang us if we turned up without one?

"Oh, very high," Spooner replied.

He had this sort of glint in his eye but eventually he revealed he had a spare tie, a very important one, a precious one, in fact the Jose Mourinho of all ties {the special one).

It had a horse on it, and some wing things coming out of it. It was an Airborne tie, the Parachute regiment, and the winged horse was none other than Pegasus. Many brave men had sacrificed everything for the honour and privilege of wearing one and indeed died in battle with the famous horse on their caps or lapels.

I certainly wasn't fit to wear it but seeing as the other lads had got sorted out, and dinner was being served, Colonel Spooner was sort of pushed into a corner, so he lent it to me on the strict understanding that as soon as I stood up to leave the table and took one step outside the room I had to hand it straight back, and not get any creases in it or drop it in my soup.

Sometimes a tie is not just a tie. What could possibly go wrong? I had worn a tie before without any great drama, so hey, shut up and let me put it round my neck. I was starving. I promised all of the above, never asking why it was so precious to him, and he never explained, despite the fact it was a Para tie. It obviously had some great relevance but I'll never know.

What I do know is, the following morning when I gave it back to him, it wasn't in quite the some condition as when he lent me it the night before. In fact it was only half the tie that he had lent to me the night before. What could possibly have happened to Colonel Spooner's tie in that short space of time? And what made him go apoplectic?

We'd had the meal and then retired to the bar for cigars and brandy, as you do. During some point, at this time, Colonel Spooner must have upped sticks and gone to bed, leaving me still in possession of his prized asset. Not realizing I was still wearing it, I completely forgot to give it back, and the Colonel, on his part, forgot to ask for it back. You can see how wars start. I blame the brandy.

You know at a certain stage of an evening when you're happily merry and it's gone midnight and you have an early start and it's time for bed, and then something in your brain says: "Fuck this, you're in one of the most exciting capital cities in the world, let's go clubbing?"

Well, it sort of happened to me, to us actually, so off we went looking for action and it wasn't too long before we found it. We walked into the first place we came across. It was a sort of dark beer Keller. Loud rock music was coming from a band on stage and the place was full of hairy-arsed bikers, probably a chapter of the Berlin Hells Angels, my sort of place.

Thick fag smoke filled the room but I eventually found the bar and got the beers in. I had two pints in one hand and two in the other. I looked round to see where the lads were. They had found a table a few feet away and were hurrying me up for their lager.

Now you know sometimes you do something and you didn't mean to do it, but by which time you have already done it? Well, just at that very same time, the band had finished playing, I looked over at the lads, clicked my heels together, raised my right arm in the air and shouted JAWOHL MEIN HERR!

Well the place went silent. I could feel many eyes burning holes into my body. It just came out, youthful exuberance I guess, or maybe I was being an arse, but I didn't mean it in any derogatory way, unlike Basil Fawlty in the German sketch.

The band struck up again, I gave the lads their beer, and it was all agreed I'd fucked up so we should skull them fast and piss off.

After a few more songs and a few more beers (it was late by now, or is that early?) and my minor misdemeanour seemed to have been forgotten, so one more for the road, then bed.

Just before we left I popped for a leek, got the little fella out and emptied my now rather full bladder, couple of shakes and back home he went. I turned round still zipping up my trousers and nearly shit myself.

There, standing in my face, at some six foot plus, was the largest, hairiest biker in Europe. Smiling, the cunt held a 10-inch knife to my throat and gave it a little shove, just to let me know it was real and he wasn't playing any games. It's not true what they say about your life flashing by you. There's no time. There's no time to think, run, fight, no time for nothing. Fear had kicked in and I was petrified, motionless, and looking death right in the fucking face.

I once had a gypsy pull a gun on me, but I was in a car. I stood a chance. The bullet might not hit me, or perhaps just graze me or even miss altogether. I got out of that okay, but this knife was actually in my throat. My hands were practically on my cock. His other hand was on my tie pulling it tight, and then he raised the blade above my head.

I was unable to move. This was about as bad as it gets. I was once again about to become my own news story. As the knife came down, I just shut my eyes. Good night God bless.

A rush of air blew passed my cheek, but I felt no pain. Shark attack victims say they never really feel the bite and it isn't until they get ashore that the pain and horror kick in. This must be what was happening. It was already black. Maybe I had died without any pain. Maybe death wasn't that bad after all?

In my still-functioning mind this entire event had taken several years, but in reality it had taken seconds. I opened my eyes. Well, what did God really look like? Now I was going to find out.

No he didn't look like a big sweaty hairy-arsed biker, so therefore I wasn't dead. I still felt no pain. How could he have missed? Well, he didn't. He wasn't after me. He wanted my tie, and he got it, well half of it anyway.

He was still standing there, still holding his knife, waiting, for fuck's sake, what did he want? He'd already sent me to my death and back. If he'd wanted the tie that badly, he only had to ask. "No problem mate, have it and here's some money too!"

Then the penny dropped. I don't think he was that pissed off at me for insulting his entire country and countrymen. This fucker actually thought I was a Para and he wanted to fight me.

I am sure if a real Para man had been in my shoes, wearing a real Para tie, then this fucker would probably have got what he was looking for. But how could I tell him it had been a terrible mistake.

He left, and I went back to the table white and unable to breath properly.

"Come on, we're going. We're going now, just move everyone, just move now, it's time to go."

I felt an arm round my shoulder. It was my new fucking friend again. This couldn't be happening. Quick as a flash, Shaun snapped a picture of us both and someone else offered to buy him a drink, all blissfully unaware of what had just happened. As matey boy's head turned, I just sprinted for the door – abracadabra and I was gone in a cloud of smoke.

A few minutes elapsed and the lads came sauntering out, talking about finding a curry house. I tried to explain, now that I was stone cold sober with fright, what had just happened, and pointed out that I had just lost half a tie to a crazed-up biker who thought I was in the forces. They all looked down at the tie, to find only a knot round my neck, and corpsed into fits of laughter, not believing a word of it. I knew Spooner was going to be none too pleased when I saw him the next morning. Fuck that, two near death experiences in two days. What had I done to deserve this?

At breakfast a few hours later Spooner made a beeline straight for me.

"Where's my tie?" he asked.

"Oh good morning Colonel, " I replied.

"Where's my tie?" he repeated.

"Oh, it's in my room, I'll get if for you after …, " I said.

But before I could get the word breakfast out, he just looked me coldly in the eyes and said in a very low controlled sort of voice: "Go and get me my tie now!"

"Yes of course, Colonel, I'll pop upstairs now, and thank you for lending it to me."

I bit my lip, and nearly asked him if I could post it back to him once I was safely back in the UK, but decided not to. I swear walking back slowly up the stairs to my room, I knew what it was like for a prisoner just before going to the gallows. I got half the tie and headed back down the stairs to where Spooner was waiting.

The lads had taken up position strategically round the foyer, to eavesdrop on the impending conversation. But there was no need. You could hear the fucker's voice all the way to the Brandenburg Gate.

I did try to explain, but sometimes in life you just have to take it on the chin. The more I said the worse it was. He really seriously could not believe that I did not defend the honour of the tie, that I just stood there and let some hoodlum just take it.

Why wasn't I dead? It just wasn't good enough.

To say it caused a tad bit of friction between the Beeb and the Army was somewhat of an understatement. The lads just loved it, and said: "Coatesy, whatever you do and wherever you go there's always a story!"

The rest of the trip went well, with people asking me every three seconds to tie their shoelace, or tie up the battery bag, or tie a knot in the cables... The finished programmes looked great, and we had a bash or two with the lads, but I never made them, as Spooner was there, and he still wanted to kill me.

In the end everyone was happy and we all got what we wanted out of it. Unfortunately Colonel Spooner died some years ago, but I am still sorry about his tie and what it meant to him. I now have my own tie.

Fish

Well, my little gastronauts, I love fish but I hate early starts. One cold winter's morning, very early – about 5ish, we met up with an up and coming chef on a frosty fish quay in North Shields.

He was plugging one of his first cook books, Floyd on Fish, and we were following the process of buying the fish straight from the boat and getting it onto the table. Keith Floyd has everything – passion, humour, comedy, personality, and is a brilliant chef to boot; in fact Floyd for me is the Daddy when it comes to cookery programmes. I love all he does and I am lucky enough to have tasted his work.

Floyd has been there, done it, caught, cooked and ate it, travelled and seen just about everything. He was doing cooking on TV before even TV was invented. He's the father of the TV chef and it's hard not to like him or indeed his food. The only issue I have with old Floydy is the fact, in my opinion, he uses too much salt. I have tried, like many, to recreate his recipes, with some success, but, like all true professionals, he makes it look so easy.

As cold mornings go, I remember it being bloody freezing – ten minutes and all your pinkies start to go numb and that's with all your thermals on. The wind chill factor at the mouth of the Tyne in winter is an experience. I believe there was a hip flask on the go, with something or other in it, purely for medicinal purposes, but it was far too early for vino.

Keith took a keen interest in us all, especially the Cameraman,

Les, my old man who indeed is a great cameraman, and I've learnt my profession from him. But Keith is no fool, and he knew that if you win the heart and mind of the man taking the pictures, you can be sure that he will pull out all the stops to make you look pretty and go that extra mile. Fuck him over and he can make you look a right twat, and sometimes we do just that when people rub us up the wrong way or treat us like a piece of shit.

To be fair, it's mainly politicians and footballers that wouldn't give you the time of day, so that's why sometimes you see them on TV, green, or under-exposed, or with an ear missing or a tie undone, or perhaps with a bogey up their nose, or a piece of carrot between their teeth. It happens all the time.

Within minutes Floyd knew our names, and what was expected of us. I, at the time, was doing the sound, so to be fair without good audio we would have been a bit fucked, as not many Look North viewers could lip read. But there was no fear of that as he had won us over, even without cooking us fish for breakfast.

Floyd, as you may well have noticed, likes to do everything in one take, which could last several minutes, if not longer. To put this into perspective, the average shot you see on Sky News lasts about 4 or 5 seconds without a cut, so you have to be on your game making sure there is a good healthy balance of presenter, food, chopping and cooking without any of those long embarrassing pauses.

On to me Les, down to the fish Les, back up to me Les, onto the herbs … it's all part of his style and it works very well. The fresh fish was bought and a restaurant kitchen was found, a few extra ingredients sorted, and off we went. I loved it, and even later on, watching his many programmes, I would loved to have taken the place of his regular cameraman Clive, instead of freezing my bollocks off outside some shitty courthouse, doing some trial. The relaxed atmosphere and exotic locations, not to mention the 5 star hotels and drinking sessions, at times makes me green with envy. But sour grapes aside, I guess once you've done one food programme, you've done them all, and maybe the predictability of them would truthfully have got to me after a while. I still have no idea what I'm doing tomorrow, where I'm going, who I'm going to meet, where I'll be staying or when I'll be back, so to be fair every day is a new adventure. Even now I still consider myself to be very lucky.

All went well with our fish breakfast. I remember tasting it, and it was exquisite. After we finished, he gave us all a signed copy of his book and thanked us all for our professionalism. He said he hoped it would look good when put to air, and indeed it did.

Back at the studios I remember shouting round the newsroom that one of the world's top chefs had just cooked us breakfast and you could stick your bacon bun up your arse!

Some years later Jue and I were having a dirty weekend away in Dublin trying to drink Temple Bar dry, when who should come walking along the street towards us wearing a white suit and Panama hat, with a beautiful lady it tow, but Mr Keith Floyd himself.

After all he'd done and the people he'd met I doubted very much whether he'd remember me or even that cold morning on North Shields fish quay. I bid him good afternoon and as he didn't seem to be in that much of a hurry, I pointed out that we once worked together. He remembered the morning with incredible accuracy, recalling how cold it had been. Even more incredible, he asked how Les was! Some guy, some chef.

NB This was written before Keith's sad death. RIP Keith. I still mean every word.

Mary's Dog

My grandmother Mary used to live in Whitley Bay and was given a Pomeranian dog due to a friend's divorce. Les had sorted it out for her – not that she actually wanted a dog. Kitty, I think her name was, and after a while they both took to each other and were a regular sight on the seafront, but my grandmother was forever complaining about people – mainly Japanese tourists – taking pictures of them both.

To be fair this eccentric Englishwoman and her small hound were quite a sight. My nan used to drag along one of those baskets with two wheels and a long handle, and when Kitty was knackered, which usually occurred at the bottom of the drive, she was placed in said basket and promenaded along the seafront.

One morning, while I was still living at home, some of the time anyway, I had several jobs to do before we set off for work, one of which was to sort the car out. This meant putting the camera, batteries and kit in, and removing sandwich wrappers, coke cans and crisp packets. At the time I was still Les's sound recordist.

The crew car was a Range Rover and on this morning as I opened the rear doors, I noticed an old flowery bag. I dragged it out of the car only to have its contents fall onto the driveway. Fucking hell, it was only a small dead decomposing dog, not just any small dead decomposing dog, but Kitty, my Nan's dog.

Kitty had died some days before and Mary had asked Les to get her cremated and bring back her ashes. Les had then tasked me to hoy the small dog in the bin and fill a small jar, which she had given him, with ashes from our open fire, which had been burning logs and fag ends with some gusto the night before. As I started filling the jar I asked my father's advice regarding exactly how many ashes would a Pomeranian dog leave, we came to the consensus two scoops, or was it three?

The ashes, sometime later were given back to my grandmother, and then put into an ornate urn and placed on her mantelpiece. Visiting my grandmother some weeks later, she seemed very pleased with her urn and Kitty's ashes. Job well done, I thought, and she was no wiser. As she left the room to get us both a cup of coffee, I took a sneaky peek inside, only to realize in horror that it contained three fag ends, two ring pulls and the cap off a Carlsberg bottle!

My nan came back into the room and noticed ash marks on the floor and my fingers, as I had made a bit of a mess while trying to quickly removed the foreign objects.

"What are you doing?" she inquired.

"Just giving Kitty a pat, Nan, " I answered.

I think she went for it, or perhaps she thought her grandson had some strange perverse obsession and got off with playing about in the ashes of dead animals, I will never know.

The Weatherman

You always knew what kind of week you'd had at the Beeb, by the weatherman. Every Friday afternoon the Look North weatherman was to be seen, pre-recorded, bringing the weekend weather forecast from an exotic North East location – rivers, lakes, mountains, stately homes or any big event that was happening over the weekend always saw the weatherman bring his forecast from outside the studio. And needless to say, he always told us it was going to rain.

Now to be the chosen one, the one with the privilege of recording said weatherman, you'd have had to really have pissed off the News Editor sometime during that week, because doing the weatherman was a punishment. The crews hated it. The bugger could be anywhere, and no one wanted to be filming him at 3 o'clock in the afternoon in Berwick-on-Tweed, a good two-hour drive from my working patch of Teesside, therefore no early finish. Therefore no early doors!

I did the weatherman quite a lot. I don't know exactly what we had done to upset the news editor this particular week, but we were sent out to film a load of young air cadets who were making their first ever parachute jumps on Newcastle's Town Moor. We did a news report on it, and then were kindly sent back later that day to do the weatherman.

Alan Doorwood was a great weatherman, one of those local

heroes you sometimes get. He even had his own fan club amongst the Tyneside students, and he knew his stuff, inside out. Thinking about it, as long as he said rain somewhere in his report he couldn't go much wrong! The cadets were put, ten at a time, in a sort of cage that was fixed to a massive helium balloon tethered to a monster truck with a great winch system and basically let go.

The cable that attached the two was about 1, 000 feet long and when they reached that height they would simply jump out attached to their fixed parachutes and were back on the ground in no time. Simples.

The News Editor that day had a great sense of humour and had arranged for us to do the weatherman in the cage dangling 1, 000 feet above Newcastle – great guy! When we arrived we knew nothing of his little jest, until some big hairy-arsed sergeant introduced himself and told us to put this on, with that he passed us all a parachute.

"You're having a fucking laugh aren't you?" we said.

"No, son, put it on. You need it, " they replied.

"OK you've had your little joke, now what's the score?" I asked.

Staring angrily at me, the sergeant ordered us to put them on, and then explained what was about to happen.

The story that did the rounds is completely untrue, as ever. Never at any time did I honestly think for one moment that we were being made to do a parachute jump with all the kit, and record the weatherman mid-flight doing a piece to camera, telling us it was going to rain at the weekend. That story is completely untrue.

But this sergeant guy was being quite serious about the whole thing. He told us that if we were in the cage and the cable snapped, we would be pushed out gently and float back to the ground. He wasn't joking. If the cable did snap 1, 000 feet up, the balloon would shoot off skywards and stop somewhere between Mars and Jupiter, so to save us from a near certain death, he would happily hoy us out, and leave us to our own devices.

There would be no point in trying to explain what we were to do in the event of a break because, as he put it, there was far too much to remember, and when the adrenaline and fear kicked in, we'd remember nothing anyway. It was easiest just to be pushed and hope for the best. He was really enjoying this, especially as Health and Safety hadn't yet been invented and risk assessment was a pipe dream.

So our parachutes on and up we went. It was all going swimmingly until the cable snapped! And we had to jump! Just joking, but I did have fucking nightmares about the whole incident – 1, 000 feet up is some drop.

Once we were up there and fully airborne, we did the weatherman in world record time. Once back on terra firma, I asked the smiley sergeant just how often the cable does actually snap? With a dry smile and knowing wink he replied, "All the time."

The smug bastard.

The Barron

The Barron's head appeared through the kitchen door, but clearly, weighing over a ton and standing at 18 hands high, he wasn't going to make the party inside. Yet Lord Fields who had spent the day hunting and drinking whiskey didn't seem to be perturbed by this small, or indeed large fact.

A small ruckus broke out as more and more of the beast was forced onto the tiny kitchen. The horse, not seeming to be too bothered, was spurred on by the party goers. The resplendent Lord in full hunting kit was calling for the hounds.

Just another incident at another famous 'Les party'. Lord Fields or Derrick, who was not actually a Lord, but had given himself the title and to be fair suited the role, had not been invited to the party. In fact, he was never invited but living in a small village the jungle drums soon got round to playing, and everyone who had been in either of the two local pubs knew after closing time there would be a good chance of some action at Les's.

Degsy (Lord Fields) was promptly given a large scotch and sent on his way, as per normal. Back to the party, and Lord Fields and The Barron were putting on Long Newton's equivalent of Hickstead at 2 in the morning.

Fences were jumped, perfectly-manicured front lawns turfed up like a Glastonbury field, bonnets of cars jumped. This for sure would end in tears, pain and possibly a prison sentence for someone.

"Fuck, fuck, fuck, stop him!" someone shouted.

"You fucking stop him!"

A row erupted.

"I'll fucking stop him, " I said.

I sometimes used to ride this mighty horse and help Derrick muck out at his stables, so I knew the score. With a bottle of scotch in one hand and a pack of fags in the other, I managed to stop the faultless round and summoned Degsy in for more ale. It worked.

The Barron, hot, sweaty and pumped up, was not invited so we tethered him to a drain pipe, that restrained him for all of three seconds before he had pulled it clean off the wall. Something more substantial was needed. Before I could say no he had been tied to the front bumper of a brand new white Lotus Esprit turbo owned by a well-known businessman, who fortunately was pissed inside the house.

The car came up to the horse's knees, and needless to say, the poor old big nag took fright and tore off up the road, pulling it behind him until bits of the Lotus started to fall off and The Barron, knowing it was well past his bedtime, headed for the hills. Les arrived outside, and asked: "Where's the horse?"

"No idea, " I replied, "gone for a trot. You'd better go get Lord Fields. It's not my problem. They're your mates, and I'm off to bed, You sort it out. I've got school tomorrow!"

The parties went on for many years and as a young teenager I thought this was the norm. There were many great and funny stories, and many days missed off school due to serious hangovers both by me and my brother. Things did slow down a bit for a while, when we found our lad seconds from death choking on his own vomit, but after a fully-clothed cold shower and a few laps round the garden, he was soon back into the swing of things. Looking back I just shudder. The innocence of youth.

Hot Date

Like every young teenage adolescent, I have had the "hots" for one or two sexy women in my time. Contrary to popular belief I have never actually stalked anyone!

One such lovely lady was the Olympic swimmer and medallist Sharron Davies. Just the sight of her in a cozzy does it for me, so when I had the opportunity to take her for a drink, it was quite literally a dream come true.

We were working at the Commonwealth Games up in Edinburgh and were the pool crew for the regions. At the time I was at the Beeb, so if any athlete from one of the local stations' areas had done particularly well or indeed won a medal, we were sent along to interview them and had to send them back the material for the nightly show.

The media village was vast, and there were crews there from all over the world. The place was buzzing, and on the track Team GB was doing reasonably well. We had a large crew up there – directors, producers, fixers and the like. We needed everyone. As I remember it was bloody hard work, long hours, but a great laugh.

This one day we headed down to the pool complex to do an interview with someone or other, and along with us came our producer Ronnie Burns, an ex Olympic swimmer himself, and a bear of a man, but with a great sense of humour, and a deep pride of his own country in hosting the games.

Sadly Ronnie is no longer with us but his stories are. Ronnie seemed to know everyone around the pool – swimmers, coachers, medics, timekeepers and not just from these isles either.

I was trying to focus on the faces and not the bodies of the female swimmers, but let's face it, it's perfectly normal for any hot-blooded male to ogle an attractive woman in a swimsuit. (A university lecturer once said that teaching female students was a perk of the job!)

Anyway, this one attractive lady was making her way with some haste towards Ronnie. She was wearing a track suit, and was literally sprinting towards him. As she came closer I remember thinking she looked like Sharron Davies. It was not until she had her arms around him and was giving him big hugs that the penny dropped – fucking hell, it was Sharron Davies!

The two of them went back some years and she was working in a journalistic capacity. I got the impression that she wasn't competing, and here she was hugging the boss. Cool!

We were all introduced and they took off together talking about swimming and stuff. We did what we had to do at the pool and set off back to the media centre. Later that evening over a few drinks I quizzed Ronnie about Sharron and as the night and the ale rolled on, I asked him what he thought the chances were of me taking her out for a drink. I believe he said something like between zero and none.

I begged him to set me up for a drink with her, not a date, not a meal or a night out, one drink, just one, ten minutes no more, tell her anything, like I was going to swim the Channel and did she have any tips. I knew he had the power to pull strings like that, and if he did, well, I'd be his best friend or something like that. He said that if I'd shut up he'd see what he could do, adding: "But don't hold your breath, sonny."

Several days had passed and I had completely forgotten about my hot date. It obviously wasn't going to happen. Besides we were so busy doing other stuff there was just no time to think about anything.

One quiet-ish afternoon during a bit of down time, a DR (despatch rider) came walking into our office with a telegram. There was nothing unusual about that, as we didn't have mobiles or pagers in those dark days, except this telegram was for the attention of one Mr Karl Coates. The hairy-arsed biker looked around the room and shouted my name out again.

I shouted back: "That's me!" and he looked a tad bewildered at someone not knowing or remembering their name, but gave me the message all the same and took off. No one else in the room gave it a second thought. It was strange, very strange. "Now what's going here then? Who knows I'm here? What can it say? Who's it from?" I wondered, smelling a rat or a wind-up. Why didn't I just open it and find out! So I did.

It started, Dear Karl and ended love Sharron x. It was allegedly from Sharron Davies, and said Ronnie had had a word and yes, she could meet me for a very quick drink that night at 7 in the cocktail bar of her hotel, but due to other commitments she couldn't stay long.

It was a wind-up, it was a fucking wind up, or was it? God, what if it was real? What if I was going to have a drink with Sharron Davies? What if she would be waiting for me really tonight, and the two of us drinking cocktails in her hotel bar? God, what the Hell should I do? I know Ronnie could well have sorted it, but I also knew he liked a wind-up, so I decided to confront Ronnie with the telegram. He was very busy typing out a script, so he was also very abrupt with me.

"Did you send this?" I asked.

"No, Karl, fuck off!"

"Is this a wind up?"

"No, Karl, fuck off!"

He stopped typing and looked up at me.

"Look, son, you asked me to sort you something out. I did, and frankly I don't give a shit what you do. I'm very busy, now piss off."

I consulted the rest of the lads who were just amazed as me with the telegram. My conclusion was: "You bastards are all in this together, or it's for real."

Dilemma time. I could go and she might not be there and I would look like a dick. Don't go and she might be there and I would miss a date with the woman of my dreams. I had no choice. My destiny was already written. I went. I told the lads I wasn't going out for a meal with them that night and would see them all at breakfast.

I scrubbed up well back at the hotel and popped out to buy a tie and some bloody expensive aftershave, and set off for her hotel, telegram in hand, and nice and early. Should I buy her some flowers, I wondered? Shit, no, it was a quick drink, not a bloody marriage proposal.

My nerves had got the better of me, and I was shaking like a leaf. My head was spinning. We all have someone we would like to have a drink with and Sharron Davies was right up there on the top of my list. In 40 minutes it was going to happen. It couldn't have been better if I'd won the pools.

I sat at the bar and ordered a beer. What if she didn't drink? Should I order a coke? No, bollocks, I needed alcohol. Across the room I could see the stairs to the lobby but only half the lift, but the bing could be quite clearly heard as the doors opened so I would have a few seconds warning. The bloody lift was in permanent use and at every bing I gave a little look, straining my neck. After a few beers, the barman just came out and asked if I was on a blind date.

"Shut up, you fool! It's no blind date, it's Sharron Davies!"

"What? Sharon Davies the swimmer?"

"Yep and she's a bit late but I'm fitting her in!"

Off he went to tell the rest of the staff and they all had a little peek in at me, just as you do to the chimps at a zoo.

The lift was binging, my neck was hurting, and the room was by now quite full, and the bowl of nuts on the bar must have been changed five times. There was no clock and I don't wear a watch, but not long now before me and Sharron got down to business. I was feeling a bit pissed (I'd had four pints). Shit, if I'd had four pints and eaten three kilos of nuts, then what time must it be?

The barman could hardly contain his pleasure when I asked him.

"Five past nine sir."

Five past fucking nine? I'll give you five past nine, you little shit, I thought. Five past fucking windup time, that's what time it was. They'd got me, hook line and sinker, the bastards. Two and a half hours I'd sat there, my nerves were shot. I was a jibbering wreck, my neck was in spasm and my pride was hurt.

Yes, of course they'd opened a book on me to see how long I'd last there, by myself, on my own, Jonny no mates. Bets were placed and money exchanged hands. They were even taking it in turns to check out the state of play by walking past one of the windows every 15 minutes before returning back to the pub over the road and pissing themselves laughing.

I just took it on the chin, yet again. Never let it be said I can't take a joke.

The rest of the games went fine and they even presented me with a medal, a gold chocolate one, for being the receiver of the best wind-up, in the best wind-up category. Thanks lads.

The Big Swim

Quite a few of my stories involve water. I have no idea why, but even to me it seems a bit strange. Most do involve water, yeast and hops! Maybe it's the fact I'm Piscean. Who knows?

I love swimming and try and get into the pool two or three times a week. In my younger days, whilst at school, I swam for the county, and I reckon I could still give any Olympic swimmer a good race over two yards, but I never had the real commitment you need – six mornings and evenings a week, and that's just to start.

Once you realise that you'll never win gold, then maybe it's time to do it just for fun. A mate at school hated swimming so much that he used to forge sick notes himself to get out of it. He wasn't the sharpest pin in the box and once wrote, "Dear Sir, please excuse Paul from swimming as he has great difficulty breathing underwater." It's true, I saw his letter.

Whilst on holiday, when I was very young, I decided that I could swim, so I took off my armbands and jumped in the deep end of the big pool. After going under for the second time I realised I was in deep shit, but, for some bizarre reason, I didn't want to call out in case I made a scene and got into trouble. Thank God I did, and was pulled out semi-conscious by my dad.

You would have thought I'd have learnt my lesson, but on a boozed-up football trip to York, I decided to swim the river, much to the delight of the rest of the team.

In this country, as we all know, the water is cold – in most cases, it's very cold, and it's normally quite common for people to suffer heart attacks due to the shock when they first get in. As I dived into the Ure my heart certainly missed a beat, yet it wasn't my heart that I was worried about – it was the pleasure craft and the tourist boats that were now unable to see me in the murky water and were obviously trying very hard to plough me over.

At this point, I'd just like to thank the lads for nicking my clothes and pissing off when I swam back, giving me the enjoyment of an afternoon walking around York in my undies. Still, having not learnt my lesson and enjoying a little flutter and a wee dram, I was once challenged to do a swim. "Coatesy, bet you can't swim the width of Ullswater and back in your state!" Game on, despite the many drowning stories I've covered over the years!

So while everyone sat round the bar drinking tinnies, I set off for a little splash. The water in the Lake District must be the coldest in the country and it's very deep. There are no warm tides or currents and, being the Lake District, there isn't much sun to heat it. It's cold enough skiing in a wetsuit on top of the water, but when you've just got your shorts on, it's a completely different matter, and to make matters worse, there's very few craft on the water to help you out if you get into trouble. It was a long swim. How is it that things don't seem so far away when you're stood on the shore, but when you're actually doing it, it goes on and on and on…

I got to the other side with only mild hypothermia, and as I climbed out my body warmed up as though I had stepped into a sauna. I caught my breath and wondered what to do next. I had long since been forgotten by the lads on the other side of the shore. I don't even think they could see me, let alone hear me if I got in to trouble. The other side of Ullswater where I was had no roads or houses, just heather and lots of sheep, who didn't seem to mind me joining them.

A quick run down of my options and I realised there was only one – I was just going to have swim back, so I set off. Things were going swimmingly well until about half way back when cramp set in and my extremities were turning blue.

When you hear in winter that old people have died because of hypothermia, it's not that they freeze to death, although some do; it's because when you get very cold, the blood in your body starts to thicken around the vital organs, heart, liver, kidneys, and then blood clots appear.

That's when the real serious problems start, and I was starting to have a real serious problem. I was slowly losing the use of my legs – not, you might think, a massive problem. Those guys in the Para Olympics can swim like fish. All the same it was becoming a real problem to me.

The human body is a wonderful thing and has many devices that kick in to keep you from death, one being a determination and will to live. I had put myself in this situation and it was up to me to get out of it. Besides I wasn't going to drown in my favourite lake. How bad would that look?

My breathing was becoming irregular and my arms were tiring. I couldn't even call out. I knew that when fear and panic both set in it's time for the big sleep and that stage was not too far away.

I had been living on adrenaline for some time and it had gone, but I was nearly there. You hear the phrase "one last push" used in all sorts of scenarios. I had one last desperate push, maybe ten seconds or so, left in me and after that the tank would be drained.

My mates had no idea what state I was now in. I could see them. I could see their faces and hear their clapping. I was feet away from the bank, but tragically that's when most drownings occur, and how often have I heard that, in my job?

I asked for a helping hand, much to the amusement of everybody. Inside I was thinking: "No, you fuckers. I am not a drama queen. I am about to die."

There was even more laughter, then a hand came out and I was saved. I was pulled out moaning like shit and given a refreshing can of Carling! Now that's what friends are for.

★ ★ ★

Another guy that had problems mid-swim was a cross-channel swimmer who was attempting the Channel, both ways. The conditions for such a swim pretty much have to be perfect and can be done only at certain times during the year when the tides are in your favour.

We had been in Dover for a few days covering the event for the Beeb, and had been up at 5am for two mornings in a row expecting him to start but the weather conditions were against him. But on the third morning he was good to go.

At about 7 he was all greased up and we set off, five of us in a tiny boat and him swimming by the side. The official Channel swimming bloke was with us and pointed out that if at anytime he touched the boat it was game over – he could be given drinks with the use of a pole, but no more.

The two-way crossing would take some 16 to 18 hours, with a brief stop for a couple of minutes on a beach in France. But mid-Channel there was a problem. This guy had pulled both his groins and now had only limited use of his legs. The two-way was off, but he was carrying on regardless, trying just to make it one way.

Brave, foolish, inspirational, call him what you will, but after 17 hours and into the following day, he made the beach in France at first light, and we were there to record it. I take my hat off to him.

The Channel at night in a small boat is bizarre. One of the busiest shipping lanes in the world, and there we were, sitting on deckchairs, and looking up at massive black shapes with small pockets of light peeping through at us; indeed somewhat of a risky business.

If you ever make a trip across the Channel at two miles an hour in a small boat at night and with practically only a sexton and the stars to navigate with, be sure you see the captain's credentials.

When we got back into port at Dover, there was a message from the boss to ring immediately. There was another job to do straight away. Not having really slept for four days we all thought it was a wind-up, but nothing could have been further from the truth. Dover is just round the corner from Deal, and the IRA had just bombed Deal barracks, with many injuries and loss of life.

"Get there, and quick!" we were told.

We did, but that's another story.

Cleveland Child Abuse Inquiry

I sometimes get asked what's the longest job I've ever been on, you would think to be on the same job for a day or two would be a long time, perhaps if it was a big news story you could be on it for 5 or 6 days possibly even a week or two as with the Shannon Mathews case, and if you were on a long complicated court case perhaps even a few months or so. We like everyone else cover the beginning of a big trial, may be a day or so in the middle if there are any juicy bits to report, and then again at the end, when the Judge sums up and the jury goes out.

Believe you me Juries are the most unpredictable body of men and woman you are ever likely to find, with some juries taking from less than half an hour to several weeks to come up with a verdict, and when after a certain length of time the judge gets bored and he can't get on the golf course he will normally offer the jury a majority decision, even then if a majority decision cannot be reached he will dismiss the jury and go for a re-trial, and all the Barristers, solicitors and officials will rub their hands together look towards the heavens wink and smile, cos now they know they will be able to afford their partners a new Bentley for Xmas. Twelve good men and true, as they say, but again I say very unpredictable, over the years I have seen many miscarriages of justice (in my opinion that is). Sometimes with overwhelming evidence, a whole host of previous convictions and no alibi, and many witnesses, the accused, even using the right to remain silent, has walked free. And sometimes they walk due to a technicality, which is another way of saying the Police and the CPS (Crown Prosecution Service), have seriously screwed up.

Again I have seen (in my opinion) innocent people being sent down. Sometimes in certain cases I am all for a few sitting judges being Judge and Jury, and I believe we will in the future see more of this. I have to be very careful here about what I say, and let me reiterate these are my own personal views and no one else's, and for lots and lots of legal reasons I shall not go into any case details, except one, and that is of the Cleveland Child Abuse Inquiry, a story that I covered for over a year, in fact for nearly two years, on and off.

It was without doubt the most boring job I have ever done, every day started with an arrival shot of the judge, Judge Butler-Sloss, I believe she was made a Dame and indeed later on a Baroness, all due to me, NOT. She deserved it, after taking on that case for so long trying to look interested and not falling asleep for over a year takes some doing, and after her arrival at court every day that my friends was pretty much it, work wise at least.

As it was an Inquiry into child abuse, and some of it was held in closed court, there was very little you could report on, no names, addresses, no ages, no charges, no reporting of almost any event. Where children are involved it's pretty much a closed shop, in case you identify any of them, and if something slips out and reported on that shouldn't, it's not unusual for the news editor or paper editor who disclosed those details via their outlets to be hauled up in front of the Beak, and given a good dressing down, it's all to do with sub judiciary laws, and you could be sent down for breaking them, as well as for breaking reporting restrictions that almost certainly occur when dealing with children.

So that was it an arrival shot of a judge every day for over a year, in fact I do recall Dame Butler-Sloss inviting us into chambers for drinkie poos at Christmas, we were after all by now on first name terms, well, Yes Marm, no Marm, when she wished us good morning, every morning as we discussed the weather.

The drinking session in her chambers turned into what I can only describe as a monumental piss up that got completely out of control, with the court ushers having to kick the door in and turf us all out, and for those that had passed out or couldn't walk a wheelbarrow was used, (JOKE), half a dry sherry and we were gone, conversation way above my head.

To sum up the inquiry quickly, two doctors kept reporting children to the local authorities who came to them with your every day illnesses, as having been sexually abused, so a case was brought and an Inquiry set up and after many many months and literally millions and millions of tax payers' pounds, the judgement was this: Yes, there may well be a problem with child abuse in Cleveland! End Of…; Year 2 was then an Inquiry into the Inquiry. I saw and heard a lot in that time that I just won't go into, but to say this, after baby P recently and Huntley, the authorities and powers that be, health professionals, doctors, nurses, police, social workers, health visitors etc, are still not working together, sharing information, or singing from the same hymn sheet, and there was, and still is, a severe lack of cooperation between agencies. This was one of Butler-Sloss's criticisms and that was in 1989.

The long old days of the Inquiry were not all doom and gloom, there were the drinking sessions, these were the days of a pie and a pint, most of the time minus the pie and most days we had a liquid lunch. Hacks were hacks and the pub the office, most afternoons were spent getting pissed by all and sundry, and the sundry often involved, barristers, solicitors and the judiciary in fact any one that wasn't due in court that day or had finished early seemed to go on a session, it really was the norm. The Inquiry was so long ago. In fact my big boss now at Sky, the Managing News Editor, a great bloke called Simon Cole (who is a smashing lovely caring wonderful boss grovel, grovel, pay rise, etc), was at the time a young ITN reporter and I remember three things about him, Firstly his tash, that he still has, secondly he was a good drinker and always got his round in and thirdly, he used to seriously hammer his expense account, as a young local Beeb lad I had never really come across these big ITN hitters, the guy even used to fly to work.

Anyway back to the bar, this one day two junior barristers were having a wager over lunch, hands were shook and the sum of a hundred guineas was mentioned, I really had no idea what or how much a guinea was I had heard the term in horse racing circles but never down a boozer in the Boro before. The bet was this, one of the barristers had bet the other that he could get the word Hippopotamus into that afternoons proceedings, with that a book was opened and many side bets were placed by all, when, what time, what would the judges reaction be, all that stuff, that afternoon the place was packed for no reason in particular!

The proceedings got under way and the bragging barrister that bet he could get the word in was speaking the conversation went something like this: Judge: "So how come in that case the child had bruising to their arms and legs?" Barrister: "Well mam I believe the child whilst running down stairs, fell over a small toy that was on or near the bottom rung." Judge: "A small toy you say, and exactly what type of small toy was on the stairs." Barrister: "I believe it to have been a hippopotamus mam," Judge: "A hippopotamus?" Barrister: "Yes mam a hippopotamus."

Little did we know at the time that he was getting a hundred guineas every time the word hippopotamus was noted into the proceedings, I even think it was true. Don't these Barristers just crack you up?

Banged Up Abroad (Not)

One of the most stupid things I have ever done is buy a large bale of marijuana from a load of gun-toting criminals in Thailand, a place where they quite happily put a rope round your neck or bang you up for life in a stinking sewer of a hell hole and throw away the key, just for having a joint. We've all seen the programmes.

I love travelling and have seen most of Europe and quite a bit of the world. Working abroad to be fair is a lot of stress, lots of gear to carry and it's long hours in countries where it's so hot, it's like working in a sauna.

But when it's on your terms, and your schedule and at your pace, I love it. I think Sky sort of know this, and I have done relatively few foreign jobs over the years. I've turned a few down and not really pushed for others. Besides there's a massive pecking order down in London, and even though we are all equal, some are indeed more equal than others. It has never really bothered me but it drives certain lads mental. Still, a few weeks in the sun once a year at their expense does me just fine.

I was going back to Thailand with my brother and our mate Shaun. When I took my year out travelling the world I spent a few months there and really fell in love with the place, and its people, its culture, its islands and beaches and also its food. So here I was again trying to cram two months into two weeks, and first stop was Bangkok. You must experience the place for many reasons, but only

65

give it a few days and then piss off to the islands. If you are going to Thailand the chances are you will fly into Bangkok anyway, so you may as well cross it off your list then.

Once you have experienced the sights, sounds and smells of this congested busy city, you will no doubt probably find yourself in the tourist streets of Pat Pong, an area of town full of bars, restaurants, brothels, sex shows and girlie boys. It's a real eye opener, and for many sad Europeans bastards, the place where anything goes, and listening to some of the tales, I mean anything. For the sex tourist it's the start of their game, but for the rest of us, a quick wander and a beer, then out!

Drugs out there are very popular with Westerners and are easily available. In fact not many foreigners actually do get strung up, because it's bad for business, and the drugs and sex trades, and this is one reason why many go to Thailand. If they started dangling a few up, the corrupt officials would be looking at the loss of millions of tourist dollars, so eyes are turned and pockets are lined and their economy rolls on.

But when Johnnie Tourist get caught with suitcases full of stuff worth millions, the authorities have to be seen to be doing something, so there's a bit of a show trial, followed by a life sentence with hard labour (when locals would be executed) and after a couple of years, there's a pardon from the King – simple – and everyone's happy.

So when we decided to buy a £5 bag of ganja to make up a couple of joints, we were hedging our bets, and the easiest way to get hold of some weed is to ask the Tuk Tuk drivers who will try and sell you everything from heroin to young girls, at the right price. Tuk Tuks are the main form of transport for tourists – they are a sort of chariot pulled along by half a motorbike with a roof, and you can get several people in. They're cheap and cheerful and just what you need to get around the crazy, crowded streets of Bangkok. In fact they are so cheap you can hire one for the night, which is precisely what we did. In the early hours, after a long drinking session, we asked our man to sort us out a bit of blow, he'd run out. We jumped in his Tuk Tuk and sped off screaming though the streets at hair-raising speed playing chicken with the oncoming cars and lorries in our search for drugs.

After ten minutes in Death Race 2000, and fearing for our lives, we decided we really couldn't be bothered any more and wanted to go back to the hotel, the aptly-named and priced Bangkok Hilton. But the driver was having none of it. There were dollar signs in his eyes and we were assured we'd be there in five minutes, which turned into 10 and then 15.

The bright lights of the city centre had well and truly disappeared. We were now in the unlit streets of the Bangkok slums. We could make out small bamboo and corrugated shacks on poles above open rivers of sewage. It soon became very apparent that this was not the place to be in the day time, never mind the middle of the night, and we were getting the sobering impression that we were getting set up.

There was no time to ponder. Out we got and we followed the driver across planks of woodern boards, criss crossing small smelly streams behind run-down shacks and tents where many families lived together.

We knocked on a door with a small hatch in it. A light appeared, locks were undone and we walked straight into a scene from The Deer Hunter. Now what the fucking hell have I got us into here?

Why hadn't we just turned around and gone back? Why do I always seem to push the boundaries of normality and get into these frightening situations? I thought, "We're all going to die!"

We were in a small dimly-lit room of a bamboo shack. Six or seven burly looking youngish Thai lads were sitting crossed-legged on the floor playing cards. A woman with a baby and some older blokes were sitting in the shadows. We couldn't quite make out their faces or their hands in the dark.

The Tuk Tuk driver started talking to some of them. We were beckoned over and instructed to sit against a back wall. The door was then bolted and locked shut, and the inhabitants changed their attention to us. There were no windows. Just one door, no escape route, and ten or so pairs of eyes giving us the once-over.

Silence. This is bad, this is very bad, I thought, and I, the old fuckwit, was responsible for whatever might happen. My heart was racing, blood pumping, adrenaline being kicked out like rain falling from the sky. Sweat poured off me like a fat pig. The room didn't seem to have any air-conditioning. My mind was turning like the proverbial whirlpool, I tried to concentrate on my breathing and not show any anxiety. Who was I fucking kidding? The look in our eyes said, "We're scared shitless. Please don't kill us."

Oh yes, we couldn't communicate. We'd become our very own news story. It would be a least 10 days before we were missed, and they'd never find our bodies. All this for the sake of a joint, and I don't even smoke the bloody stuff.

The eye contact was amazing and so was my pulse rate. I promised myself all sorts of things I would and wouldn't do again if we managed to get out of this, unscathed. These lads were not your average kids on the block selling a bit of weed to the odd tourist. They were hard core, and we were shit-scared.

Just as we were about to empty our pockets, hand over our watches, wallets and passports and plead for our lives, our Tuk Tuk driver spoke. Through his broken English and bad breath he was trying to find out just how much stuff we wanted, and what sort of stuff we wanted. They may be thinking we have come for a couple of kilos of heroin. All we really wanted was enough weed to make up three joints, about two quids' worth. But if we asked for that, we would get our throats cut for sure. Yet if we bought too much and got caught, we would be going back to the wrong Bangkok Hilton.

In the end I waved my arms about a bit and threw some money onto the floor. I've no idea how much. I didn't look but I hoped it would be enough. The room erupted into quite chatter. I think one of the other lads threw some money down as well. In fact, I think we threw down all the cash we had on us, with the thought – just take it and let us live.

Someone opened the locked door and pointed for us to leave. Right ok, here goes, I thought. Once we're out the door, I'd just fucking run like hell, but would the others follow? And where would we run to? That didn't really matter right now. What if we all got split up, and never saw the other two again? How would I explain that away to my parents? They'd say, "You left your brother WHERE?"

When we all got outside, the Tuk Tuk man told us to wait two minutes, but we all started walking, not looking back. Where's the Tuk Tuk gone? I tried not to scream. It had moved round the corner.

The Tuk Tuk man looked confused. We'd asked him for drugs and he'd supplied us with drugs. After we paid for the drugs, we didn't want them, some drug dealers we are!

As we got in the Tuk Tuk, two lads came racing towards us. Shit, this is it. They didn't want to kill us in the house. It would be too messy. They're going to shoot us in the street, in the pitch dark in a slummy area of down town Bangkok. I could just see the headlines, and it was all my stupid fault. No one would really care as we got what we deserved.

Now you're going to die Coatesy, I thought. They were on us in a flash. There was no escape. I don't know what the Thai is for "You forgot this" but as a hand appeared inside the carriage, that's what they said, and instead of a hand gun, as I had been expecting, a very large package wrapped in newspaper was thrown in. That's the drugs then, I thought. Of course! How foolish of me to forget them! How could I have been so absent-minded?

We pulled off, all alive and with what we had set out to achieve, maybe with a bit more of what we had set out to achieve, but hey! Job accomplished.

Two minutes down the road at what looked like a river crossing, the whole package was thrown into the drink! I didn't even open it. I didn't care what was in it. I didn't care if it was full of drugs or not. It was gone. We were clean and, more importantly, we were still breathing.

Getting back to the right Bangkok Hilton, the Tuk Tuk driver looked even more perplexed when we didn't have the package with us. Maybe he thought we were so desperate for drugs we had just eaten the contents there and then in the back of his Tuk Tuk. Whatever he thought, I'd learnt my lesson.

Remember boys and girls, drugs in foreign countries and Johnnie Tourist do not mix. So don't! My brother Jonny and Shaun have never forgiven me. So – sorry again.

My Gap Year

I had been on this planet for all of 21 years, and in my 21st year things started to go a bit tits up; in fact things went very tits up.

At the time I was living everywhere. During the week I would stay in my flat in Newcastle, or if I wasn't renting at the time I would doss down at my mate Shaun's house. Shaun was the cameraman I was working with at the time.

Weekends I would spend down Teesside. Friday and Saturday I would spend drinking in the Vane Arms in the village I used to live in, or down the town. Any of the towns near me were fair game. Sundays I would spend at Julia's house, so I never really knew where I was or what I was doing. No mobile phones in those days, dear boy, and I would have many messages left on other peoples' phones for me.

One night while staying at Shaun's, I had my car nicked. It was subsequently involved in an accident with a police car. It sounded a bad smash by all accounts, but the driver had done a runner. Because I hadn't reported my car stolen (due to the fact that it had gone in the middle of the night and I hadn't known it had been stolen) all eyes of suspicion turned to me.

The bobbies had been round to the Beeb looking for me, but I was still in bed. Of course, when I did realise it was gone I reported it straight away, and was asked to go straight down the cop shop for a little chat. They believed my story, that I was indeed asleep in bed, and that I could prove it, they bloody well checked it out anyway, cheeky bastards, but I guess they were only doing their job.

But as for my car, my pride and joy, it was a mess. Generally speaking, if it's going to cost half of what your car is worth to put right they will normally write the car off, and get you a nice new one, but my repair costs were about two pence under the cost of half of the car. So they just bodged it back together, and my Cavalier SRI 130 never really looked the same again. In fact when the copper showed it to me I nearly cried but he wanted to know if I'd unplugged the speedo. Now would I have done such a dishonest thing! Absolutely not!

Sometimes when cars are stolen for bank jobs or robberies the speedo is unplugged, so the police can't work out how many miles the car has done before the crime, and it makes it hard for them to pin down its movements. That is, of course, if the owner knows the correct mileage of the vehicle, so that's what must have happened in this case then. My car was going to be used in a blag!

So that was all great fun trying to sort out. I used to drink in the BBC club in Newcastle – great cheap beer, great people, great crack (I mean the laughs and not the drug). A thoroughly good night was had, playing pool and being daft! The club used to do themed nights and one night they did a Greek one. The BBC club has now closed down, due to the pissed-up employers drinking subsidised ale provided by the good licence payer, in the form of taxes which, if not paid, by said licence payer, will mean a short spell in choky. It's a crime really – if you don't subsidise my pint, they'll put you in prison. Seems perfectly fair to me! In fact, I used to find it an honour to drink your hard-earned cash away. Bollocks to the kids' new shoes, what about my pint! God, am I really getting that cynical? I'll be buying the Daily Mail next!

Anyway, this one Greek night in the club got a tad out of hand. Well, what do you expect, giving cheap subsidised Ouzo (that's enough now) to all and sundry. It's only a matter of time before it all kicks off and it did. There had been a few fights previous, then this chap accused me of something or other whilst in the gents. I decided not to punch his lights out there and then, due to the fact of not wanting to shit in one's own nest.

So I advised him that if he wanted a bout of the Old Queensberry Rules we should go outside, off the Beeb's property. He dropped it and I went back to drinking that lethal brew. The night wore on and chummy mate, who was the brother of a director working there, decided it was time for a fight. Game on! He was a tiny little shit, and as I followed him out of the building, I decided to give him a little tickle there and then.

I don't feel good about what I did and take no satisfaction from it, but the red mist had come down and that was that. The boys in blue were back at reception the following morning asking for another little chat with me but I was on the road. Later that day, I went to the cop shop and was promptly arrested for ABH. I pleaded provocation which it fucking well was, but hey, I hit him first so I got the blame. I didn't know he had just spent hundreds on dentistry, and would need the same again to put right.

The copper told me, after having my photo taken and my finger prints recorded, that if I'd kicked him they would have done me for GBH, and I may well have gone down. Why would I have kicked the fucker when he was down? Thank God I didn't.

Still, ABH is not quite like not coughing up for a parking ticket. The trial kept being re-dated and postponed. I rang and apologised to the lad concerned, even offering him a pile of cash but he wanted his pound of flesh and he got it. A severe bollocking, a discharge and a criminal record for life. The Beeb were none too pleased either and I had another little cosy chat, this time with management. I nearly lost my job, but as such a loveable character they gave me another chance.

Due to the old pals' act it never made it into the media. It never made the papers, and the whole incident was hushed up and forgotten. Ta to those concerned; for that I owe you one.

The shit was hitting the fan left, right and centre. Little did I know I was about to experience the worst time in my life. I had just been involved in another car accident, my third in as many years.

The first was when we ploughed into the side of a Nissan Micra that had just pulled out on us – I wasn't driving. The second was when I was racing a Escort XR3 and took him by overtaking on a bend, then lost it, stuck it into a wood, totalling the car, and getting out via the windscreen. The third time was in a car that had just totalled the back of another one. We all came to an understanding and pissed off quickly before the boys in blue turned up. I wasn't driving this time, but it just seemed to be one thing after other. Maybe it was time to fuck off? The seeds of uprooting and getting away were now embedded in my mind; as to where and how, I had not sorted that out yet.

My 21st birthday was just round the corner and I had planned the mother of all parties. A hundred odd people were told to meet at the local at 6pm one Saturday night, in fancy dress and that's all they knew. It had taken months of planning and cost me a fortune, and the excitement and secrecy was doing my head in.

The plan was for everyone to turn up on time have a few drinks in our local, The Vane, then three large coaches would turn up and take everyone to a place called Grosmont on the North York Moors. We would board a steam train, that I had hired, head to Pickering, where I'd booked a pub, have a party, buffet and disco in the pub, then some time later we'd do the journey back.

The coaches and the pub were easy enough to sort out, but hiring a steam train didn't prove to be that easy. For a start, it wasn't running at that time of year, there was no bar, or music on board, so we had to sort that out, and the problems just kept coming, as did the cost.

But at long last it was all in hand, and I have many people to thank for making it happen. My best mate at the time was Mac, Ian McAlpine. He lived in the village for many years and we were at primary school together. We both went to different secondary schools and at 17-ish we got it together again, going drinking, to night clubs, having weekends away and holidays in the Med, sharing beds while he laid some bird, with me out for the count.

To be fair he wasn't a great drinker and used to do a lot of driving to the clubs. Mind, he had the use of his dad's car with free petrol, and his dad's cars were always a bit tasty, normally high-powered saloons. Over the years we came very close to totally wasting a few, but we never did.

I did let him in on my secret party – how could I not? He was as excited as me and we had many arguments about what to wear, Batman and Robin, but who would be Batman? Superman, Spiderman, bank robbers, nurses, doctors, but the decision was taken out of our hands. Needless to say, we had left everything to the last minute and not realised that a hundred or so other people would clear out every costume store in our area.

So we settled on being a couple of Cavaliers, wearing hats with feathers in them, bright tunics and bloody stockings with black shoes with bows on them. Ian thought we looked a couple of right tits. I, however, thought we looked rather dashing like Ollie Reed and Michael York in the Three Musketeers. I was Reed! Cavaliers, Musketeers, what the hell, there'd be a lot worse outfits than ours, and there was.

Jue had got herself a little Indian squaw outfit, but the wig let her down. My dad Les had a birthday a week or so after mine, so to share the cost I'd said he could share the party as well, and that would mean quite a lot of media chums turning up and they knew how to party!

The day came and all was sorted. It was a great turn out and every imaginable super hero was there. Kings, Queens, judges, polar bears, you name it and someone was wearing it. There were at least 3 SS officers there. At that time you could dress up as you wanted and not be hung out to dry for polical correctness, unlike Prince Harry!

It was an instant party. Everyone was up for it and in no time at all the buses showed up. People had no idea what was on the cards. We all jumped on the buses and headed to venue two. George, Mac's dad, turned up to see us off, but we couldn't persuade him to join us.

It was early March and cold, and as the light was beginning to fade we arrived at the little picturesque station in Grosmont. After getting off the coaches we made for the platform, and there under full steam ready for the off was this enormous steam train with three carriages, and a bar and music that we had wired up earlier in the morning. Peoples' faces were a picture; the ante had just been upped. This was indeed some secret, this was indeed some party.

We all boarded. Toot, Toot, and off we went. It was great. After about 40 minutes we arrived in Pickering and I ushered everyone off the train. Walking through the small market town, we must have looked a sight. I found the pub. We piled in, hit the bar, then the buffet and then the dance floor. As with all things that you are enjoying time speeds up and that's a fact.

By now I was hammered. We were hammered, but having a crazy time. Walking back to the train for our return trip, it was freezing, but not many people felt it; you never do when you're minging.

The train was trundling back slowly, very slowly in fact. There was ice was on the rails and it was having a hard time going up the steep gradients, but hey the longer it took to get back the longer the party.

At one point the train was going at walking speed and the thought of jumping out for a snowball fight in the fields was discussed. Someone who obviously was not that pissed had pointed out that sooner or later it would speed up again, and we would be stuck. Who says alcohol clouds the mind?

The party on board was mental. All sorts of stuff was kicking off. I was drinking pints of Jack Daniels, mixed with God knows what, and was two sheets to the wind. The ride back was cloudy and still is, but I remember Mac asking me if I was going up on the roof of the train, have a bit of a surf and then climb back in through the opposite window of the one he'd just gone out. There were a few doing it, and the idea did cross my mind, but I was having trouble standing, never mind climbing and quite quickly dismissed the idea, and let them get on with it. I should have said something. Maybe I did. I can't remember.

It was my 21st birthday party and it was brill, I was pissed and everyone was enjoying themselves. Someone pulled the emergency cord. The train's brakes slammed on and all hell broke loose. My first reaction was that I would be in deep trouble now with the railway people, but certain people were panicking, creating a real scene. Somebody had seen someone come off the roof. It soon became clear it was Mac. The train stopped and we went looking for him, but the train had gone a great distance since the cord had been pulled, and no one knew quite what to do.

A good family friend at the time was a copper named Ces, ironically dressed as a judge. He came out of character and took control of the situation, for which I am most indebted to him. He got everyone back on the train and literally in a few minutes we were back at the station. It was not until everyone was in the car park that I was told what had happened.

Mac was on the roof of the train with someone else and they had shouted a warning that a bridge was coming up. The other bloke ducked down but Mac never heard the warning, or was too slow to react. We will never know. Mac died instantly.

The news spread first that he was involved in some sort of accident, and then that his body had been found. People began fainting and passing out. How could my best mate die at my 21st party? Nothing made sense. I was numb. I still am at times and not a month goes by without me thinking regularly about him.

Would we still be mates? Would he have kids? Who would he have married? His parents George and Margaret and his brother Scott are truly lovely people and I hope they don't mind me writing about this episode, as it changed my life, and how I live it.

There was an inquest, and ironically the media were knocking on my door for the story. The day before the funeral I completely lost it, and smashed up Les's house, breaking most of the bones in my hand from hitting the walls.

I have never spoken about this in over 20 years to anyone, cos it's not their business, and I still find it hard to do so.

It was time to move on and move out, and to just go. I sold up everything I had; that is, my car! I told Jue I'd see her in Australia in six months' time if she wanted to, and I fucked off, not really caring if I came back.

The Industry

A bit of advice for all you media student people out there wanting a career in news – don't bother! Really. I'm not scaremongering. Change courses now, or look to do something else because the news industry has gone tits up. The only outlets that do news properly and professionally are the BBC and Sky News. ITN has a small number of dedicated crews and takes most of its news from the local regional news programmes, and it shows.

The BBC was the last bastion of professionalism in broadcasting news, the market leader, perhaps at one point the best broadcaster in the world, and to be fair their news outlets are very good. They are our main, indeed only, competition.

Their big downfall is bureaucracy, if a plane is falling out of the sky and about to crash, the Beeb would have a meeting. Who would be on camera one, which SAT truck would they use, who would produce it, which outlets would take it, which reporter would anchor and who would report? Perhaps this is a bit unfair but having two family members that work for them and indeed I used to, I know how it works.

But I still love the Beeb. It's where I first started and I am sad to see the decline in its very high standards, especially in local news where anything goes even when it's not broadcastable. The SKY way, on the other hand, is to just do it and ask questions later.

Regional News is starting to be wound up. You must

understand that there is, and never will be, any money to be made out of covering the news. For example, covering the Asia Tsunami that hit on Boxing Day a few years back, wiped out the entire foreign budget for the year in just a few weeks.

The cost of covering wars, natural disasters and major news events is a seriously expensive business. Hotels, flights, meals, overtime, car rental, clothes, and buying stuff you need on the ground all mounts up. Sometimes you have to hire helicopters and planes, and pay for security when needed, and of course when things are scarce and demand high, things go up, especially hotel rooms. One night you might pay £80 or £90 for a room and the following night it may be £400 or more. I think it's called market forces but before you do all that, you need the kit, camera, mics, lights, laptop, edit gear, SAT truck, and so on and all the personal insurance to use it, and fix it when it goes wrong.

If I was to set up as a freelance tomorrow with all the trimmings, car and kit, I would be lucky to have change out of £50 grand depending what camera and lens I went for. Then, of course, you need to use it, and that's where reputations and contacts come in. You might also want to insure it as well, but if you're planning covering war zones, visiting nuclear establishments, covering riots or using it in extreme conditions, don't bother, because you won't get any insurance. On the other hand, you could buy a cheap £800 mini DV camera and give it to some old long-in-the-tooth reporter and tell them to get on with it, because they're now a cameraman as well! Unfortunately that's what's happening, not just at the independent TV companies but also at your regional BBC ones as well, and it doesn't look good.

The thing is, they're not very good, and they never entered the industry to be a cameraman, and a few guys I know resent it. It really is that bad. My patch in the North East is pretty representative of what's happening nationally.

Border TV – a great little set up covering Cumbria and the Borders – has gone; no more news, everyone's out of a job, the studios closed. YTV, Yorkshire Television, cut in half. Things are so bad there they've even given presenters cameras and kicked them out on the road; same with Granada TV. Tyne Tees TV, chopped in half, and lost a studio that used to broadcast to the south of the region. As with YTV, all their satellite offices and opt-out programmes are gone. It's sad and makes me fucking angry how people could be treated like this.

My phone rings from lads trying to get freelance work, but there just isn't any. Nobody – and I mean nobody – has got any money. The TTTV and YTV lads genuinely do not know if they'll have a job this time next month. I even know one cameraman who's now fitting kitchens, and another who delivers parcels.

The newspapers are just as bad – readership declining, local offices closing, people being made redundant. I too am responsible for this. If you want the news, just look on the Web. The problem is no one's worked out how to make any money from websites yet, and if they start charging for Web content, you just simply click to where they don't.

SKY and the BBC have seen this coming and our websites are just as important as the Channel itself. Some say in the next five years 50% of viewers will be watching online even more. That's the way forward, even for old school like me. Get your head round it, and if you have any problems, just ask your kids – any over three should be able to help.

When I were a lad and first started, we had no mobiles, no pagers – just pigeons and a very dodgy radio set-up. Then pagers and mobiles came in. Can you imagine now finishing a job and having to find a payphone to ring the office to find out what was next?

I remember sitting in the crew car and listening to someone talk on one of the first mobiles, to a friend in the States. It just blew me away. How did that happen then – you're doing 70 on the A1 talking to someone in Florida!

My kids just laugh when I tell them stuff like that; in fact my youngest has never felt a vinyl record, or pulled one out of a sleeve! He would have no idea how it works or what to do with it, but now technology is advancing so fast it's hard to keep up with it.

My camera is solid state; we input material into the laptop via a card reader and after you have edited it, you simply email your package to London and watch it on air. It's mind blowing when you think about it. I know what to do but don't ever ask me how it works.

If I wanted to, and I could quite easily do it right now. I could get the camera and laptop out of the car, plug it in and broadcast via SKY to the world whilst sitting in my living room, and my kids don't understand how I don't understand how this is all possible!

On several occasions I have seen news items consisting entirely of mobile phone footage, so now we're all cameramen and women, and as technology progresses with more mobile phones in the world than people, almost every news event anywhere will be captured and put on our screens in some shape, way or form. It's exciting, frightening and sad all at the same time.

I say this with a heavy heart, but I'm glad I entered the industry at the right time. Never in a career has an industry changed so much in such a relatively short period of time and I have seen and experienced it all. I have no idea where it will end; no one has.

The news agenda has changed forever. I have seen, been and experienced things that most people will never believe. I have met all people from all walks of life, from tramps to Bishops. I have worked with some great people and been given opportunities that, looking back now, I can hardly believe. I have so many people to thank for helping me on my way. I have had a great life and a great career. Truly, I have been in the right place at the right time.

The Monkey Mayor

Sometimes in life the truth and indeed the facts are hard to believe. On numerous occasions, I have come away from doing a story scratching my head, wondering what the hell that was all about, but this particular job really does take the biscuit.

But first a quick history lesson. During the Napoleonic Wars a ship went down off the coast of Hartlepool with the loss of all hands. However there was a survivor, a monkey, so the good people of Hartlepool put the monkey on trial for spying. It was duly found guilty of being a French spy and hanged. To be fair it gave little evidence in its defence! From that day the people of Hartlepool have been known as monkey hangers, which of course they are.

Back to the present, Hartlepool United football team have a monkey as a mascot. He's called H'Angus. H'Angus comes out before every home game to an AD/DC song. DC's guitarist is called Angus, which sounds a bit like H'Angus so the fans adopted it – daft, but there you go.

Anyway for the first time ever the Government and local authorities decided to elect an independent Mayor, a man or woman that the people would choose to represent them, one of their own to stand up and speak out on their behalf, a man of the area, for the area. And so the hunting began to find such a man, if indeed he actually existed in Hartlepool.

All the usual suspects and political parties put their person forward and so did a certain Mr Stuart Drummond, the Hartlepool mascot, the man in the monkey suit, the one and only H'Angus. It was meant to be a bit of laugh. On the campaign trail with Drummond was as crazy as I have ever seen. He was dressed in the monkey outfit, morning, noon and night and his only manifesto pledge was a promise of a free banana for every child in Hartlepool!

It certainly brought a bit a spice to the event, with all the politicians taking things very seriously, doing media interviews left, right and centre and stressing just how important this was for democracy.

I remember one cold and rainy campaign day with Drummond. He was sitting in the back of my van and I asked him, "What if you actually win? What is H'Angus becomes Mayor?"

Needless to say I was laughed off. Drummond did say that in the unlikely event he did get in, it would be the mother of all parties, as you could do a lot with 55 grand, which is what the new Major was going to be paid for doing the job.

Polling day came and the results of the duly-elected Mayor came in. H'Angus won! Politics in Hartlepool was at such an all-time low, they actually voted for the mascot of Hartlepool United, and now he would become their new duly-elected Major. This was not a Hollywood script, although it should have been.

Would you believe it? On Friday morning Drummond was unemployed, living at home with his mum and dad, and getting 80 quid a week for dressing up in a monkey outfit, and on Monday morning he had his own office in the Town Hall, and people were calling him "Mr Mayor". Had the world gone mad?

The following day was one of those moments you live for. Robin from the Sun newspaper was dressed in a monkey costume. Bananas were on the table at the press conference. It was indeed

Catergate: Mike
Neville and
Jimmy Carter

Shaun, Alan and
Me on Ark Royal.
Sadly Alan's no
longer with us

Easington Miner's Strike (I was upgraded
shortly after this picture was taken)

Jue and me on our
wedding day

Me and my boys

Love the suit Ken

Raquel with *that* dress
and legs – wedding

Another posy shot,
Jonny, Me and Ten
Bellies (Baz)

Letting off steam,
on board HMS
Newcastle, Kosovo

The lads at some court case

Balloon and parachutes

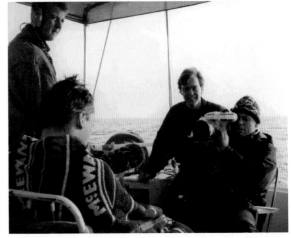

Mid Channel,
this guy had just
swam to France

Cleveland Child Abuse
Enquiry, there's not
many of us left

Sorry, I thought this
was the hire car!
Fun and games in
the US

Hallbeck Hall Hotel,
falling into the sea

I promise you this was not posed

I'm in there somewhere: a trip along the wall

Another busy day outside court

Gazza on his way to court and a good bun fight

A bit too close to a cluster bomb

Chilling out in Thailand

Trainee
miner, on a
job with Les

Me, Jonny,
Mum and Jue

Sent this sucker down like the Titanic

Flying high –
again

A fully loaded
A10, the wart hog

KATE ADIE ALERT STATES

KATE ADIE ALERT STATE BLACK:
At Black, there is a **POSSIBILITY** that Kate Adie **MAY** come to the Theatre.

KATE ADIE ALERT STATE BLACK ALFA:
At Black Alfa information has been received that there is an **INCREASED LIKELIHOOD** that Kate Adie will come to theatre.

KATE ADIE ALERT STATE AMBER:
At Amber, specific, evaluated information has been received that there is a **SUBSTANTIAL** threat of Kate Adie arriving in theatre.

KATE ADIE ALERT STATE RED:
State Red is issued as a warning of the **IMMINENT** arrival of Kate Adie in theatre. State red will remain in force until Kate Adie has left the theatre.

THE CURRENT ALERT STATE IS:

STATE RED

This war has
now got serious

Me as Bill Sykes in Oliver

Doing a turn with Iron Maiden in Spain

Train record, N'cle to KX in 2h and 19 mins

Me, a monkey
and someone
in a gorilla suit

Cockermouth
flood rescue

Another day freezing my balls off

By the Panama Canal

A quick splash in the Channel

The cartel, Les, Jonny and me

Robbo and Lamb, just before we were hoyed out

No idea why we are stood on a beach

My patch just got bigger

Very wet at the
Somme, France

Di on a visit

Inside
Flyingdale's
golfballs

Blair's last day – please don't leave us, Tone!

The Metric Martyr

Me, Gazza and Nobby, during 'happier times'

Who needs reporters?

Playtime: me, Mark and Paul

The artist – move over, shark boy

pure madness, but just how was Drummond going to play all this? Was a man in a monkey suit really going to sit in an office in the Town Hall dressed as a monkey, demanding the kids of the town be given bananas?

Drummond had been nobbled by the Labour party, and at the press conference, he insisted it was all a play, and that indeed he was a very serious candidate, with a serious message and H'Angus was just a gimmick.

Mandelson, the local MP, had got his nails into him and tried to give him 10 minutes of media training of what to say and how to say it. It didn't work. He was torn to shreds. The hounds on that morning did catch their quarry, and the young Mayor upped sticks and pissed off out the room rather sharpish after the first few questions.

He was hotly followed by the pack. We basically wanted to know why he now had changed his story and become such a lying bastard. It was all a bit embarrassing for everyone, especially the boy Drummond who would now have to learn to be a Mayor and fast.

Unfortunately Stu is still one of the lads and likes nothing better than a few beers with the boys and hanging out in lap-dancing bars, as we all do, but you would have thought that somebody might have pointed out to him that perhaps stuffing fivers down the front of some Estonian teenager's thong is possibly not the sort of thing that someone in high office should be seen doing, especially the Mayor.

Oh Stu, you couldn't even keep your campaign promise of a banana for every child in Hartlepool!

But most bizarrely of all, having kept an eye on him over the years, he actually seems to be doing a good job, even to the extent of being voted in for a third term. To be sure he gives everybody hope.

We'll never know just how much power he has or hasn't got, and only Stu will ever really know the inside story of H'Angus, but hey, it just goes to show what you can achieve if you put your mind to it. I'm not really sure what this tells you about politics or how people really think, maybe it's just a Northern thing, but now every time I pass Hartlepool going up the A19, I piss myself laughing. Monkey Hangers!

Gazza

He was the most famous hellraiser football had ever seen, both on and off the pitch. The stories are legendary, the man immortal, but the real Paul Gascoigne has never really been understood.

He made headlines on both the front and back pages, even now years after his playing days are over he still makes the front covers, making the papers millions, and bewildering his supporters.

He is a writer's dream, helping England to victory one day and then overshadowing it with his off-the-field antics the next. He will go down in history for lots of reasons.

The ball skidded along the wet soggy ground towards me at some pace, not sure whether it was meant for me or the cameraman or more likely his camera, but fortunately I had the skill of Maradona, and the feet of Ronaldo to pluck it out of the air, control it and pass it back – or did I just dream that last bit?

It was Gazza who, at 17 or 18 and slim in face, was the most buoyant, energetic footballer I had ever seen. It was the first time I had met Gazza, a young wannabe, who was just breaking into the team at Newcastle United, and tongues were starting to wag which is why we were there to interview him. In fact he wasn't much younger than me, and from that day on I took an interest in his career and then, like the rest of us, in his personal life.

The first time Gazza punched me was at his sister's wedding, a big limo event in his native Gateshead, and of course the media were there in force.

Limo after limo arrived and then Gazza got out of one. There was, as we call it in the trade, a 'bun fight' or as I've heard say a 'goat fuck'.

Anyway it was all kicking off around him – bouncers, media, punters the lot, then Gazza went past me. I pride myself at getting the pop shot and was at the centre of said bun fight. He swung a punch at me, hitting the view finder and clipping my cheek. The punch was badly placed, but my first reaction was, "What a twat!"

It was all over in seconds – from him getting out the car, through the scrum, to the church. I knew the pictures would be unusable; the bastard had just knocked the camera off my shoulder.

There was the usual commotion when the snappers and crews find out who got what, or more importantly who missed what, and whose boss would be watching the other channel to see what his lot had missed, which happens daily. Then I noticed two girls, about 18, laughing and giggling. One said, "I grabbed his arse as he went past me."

One of these idiots had grabbed his arse, the he'd turned round, seen me and thrown a punch. I would probably have done the same.

It's not unusual for certain sections of the media to provoke celebs to get a reaction. You see them leaving clubs and fighting all the time. But take away the photographers and you'd have no pictures. Everyone's playing cat and mouse, an interesting game that I stay well clear of.

The second time he gave me a tickle was when he was drinking at his local club in Dunston, a working men's club, as we have up North – no lasses, just beer, darts and doms. I think lasses are allowed in on a Saturday night or for special occasions.

Stalked by the media, he was so pissed off that he offered £50 for any camera or indeed cameraman that got fucked over. The place erupted in seconds. We were now the hunted. Gazza, Jimmy Fivebellies and his merry men set to work with some vigour at the set task.

It was bedlam and we lost, quite a lot at that. There were a few A+E visits that night.

I have done many things with Gazza over the years, and recently spent the afternoon with him and his family doing a half hour for Sky which I believe was the most viewed item on the website ever!

He opened his heart literally, revealing for the first time how his heart actually stopped due to his excesses, and many personal details about his life. Whatever you may have heard, read or seen about Gazza, one thing is for sure. He was the most gifted footballer of his generation, and I wish him well.

Canoe Man

We got a call one bright sunny morning to go to Seaton Carew. Apparently some guy had walked into a police station in London complaining of amnesia. He thought he was a missing man from the town, so we were asked to go and check it out.

That man turned out to be John (the canoe man) Darwin, and little did we know at the time but this story was to take us half way round the world. John Darwin was financially up shit creek, so he faked his own death to collect the insurance money, helped by his lovely wife Ann. This involved paddling out to sea in his red canoe, coming ashore and pushing said canoe back into the drink and making it look like he'd fallen out and drowned. Actually Ann picked him up several miles further along the beach.

The scam worked, the insurance paid up and even the Coroner agreed that John Darwin was dead. Meanwhile John and Ann went to live happily ever after in the central American country of Panama under assumed names.

There was, in fact, a lot more to the story than that. It only really broke big time when one of the papers got a photo of John and Ann in a property dealer's office in Panama city, after they had just bought some land. Someone recognised them and then slowly but surely their lies were unwoven by the media, and especially Sky.

Cleveland Police were their normal dynamic selves at looking into this crime, by just sitting back and letting the media boys crack it for them, which of course we did. It was truly fascinating. It was the lead story for some seven or eight days before being kicked off top spot, and only topped, I believe, in coverage, by the terrible events of 9/11, so in broadcasting terms it really was some story.

TV crews, documentary crews and even movie teams all piled in to Seaton Carew for a sniff around, which by now had being renamed Seaton Canoe. The locals still call it that today. The events that did unfold were amazing. Even more amazing was that this story was right on my door step, and I was enjoying every minute of it.

Firstly we acquired pictures of the Darwins at a wedding reception, then we tracked down his Range Rover (John's pride and joy) complete with personalized number plate and bought that as well. We were doing such a good job that the boss sent us out to Panama to cover that angle of the story.

Panama was pretty much as I had expected it to be, though I hadn't quite anticipated the heat and 100 percent humidity. Darwin had bought some land on the route of the Panama Canal and was trying to set up, believe it or not, a canoe school. The jungle along the route was pretty dense and am sure the silly bastard had not no idea that there were some pretty big crocs in there as well.

The people in the surrounding villagers were very friendly and the story of Darwin interested them as much as it did us back home. History of the Panama Canal was truly riveting. We got some great material which was to be used in our news reports and part of a documentary.

Our guide was some old bloke called Tom who was put there to keep an eye on things by the Americans, ex-CIA, who basically never left our sides. He was a walking History lesson and even more fantastic, an American football fan. Fortunately I was a bit into the old Grid Iron many moons ago, and could just about hold my own. He even took us to meet his son and chums at a sports bar where we watched a game and drank some Bud.

The picture that gave the game up for the Darwins was taken in a property developer's office. His name was Mario and he was truly blown away with the number of British media knocking on his downtown office door. We spent some time with him and his lovely wife and baby, and he gave us a great insight into the life and times of John and Ann in Panama.

The media circus around the trial was also great and ended with John putting in a guilty plea and Ann pleading not guilty. She was found guilty and sent down for six and a half years and John – because of his plea – got six years.

Even in prison John was trying to sell his story, sneaking bits out, but Sky News put a stop to that. I'm sure that when he gets out he won't go hungry. Who says crime doesn't pay?!

The documentary was put forward for an RTS award. The Royal Television Society awards are gongs handed out by the media to the media to keep everyone happy, but we didn't win.

We were then nominated for a Bafta. The highlight of most people's careers is to be awarded a Bafta; even getting nominated for one shows great recognition in their field. But we didn't win that either. It's a shame because we should have won both. Sky likes its gongs and we should have had two. Even more of a shame is the fact I didn't get asked to either event; mind you, I only shot half the documentary.

The Actor

One of my favourite films is Oliver Twist and one of my favourite actors is Oliver Reed. I sometimes think of the ultimate drinking session and who you'd want there. There would be me, of course, Olly Reed, Ozzy Ozbourne, Keith Moon (drummer and hellraiser of out of The Who), Richard Harris and Richard Burton, some session!

I digress. My sister-in-law Karen is really big into Am Dram, amateur dramatics, and for the summer season the Ormesby Players, where she struts her stuff, were doing Oliver Twist. I had dreamed about putting on a play and me playing the lead role, but I never thought I'd ever be given the opportunity to unleash my acting talents on the masses. Like most things in my life, it was a bit strange how it came about.

One evening out of the blue, Karen rang and explained that they were looking for a Bill Sykes and how would I like to audition for it? Thank you, good night, not interested, even through Olly Reed was my ultimate drinking partner and had played the role in the film. (There were a few versions, but Olly Reed's one is the best.)

But acting, well, I didn't think I'd have the bollocks or indeed the time, and with all those kids, the patience as well. One night, I'd sank many beers with my mate Kev, whose daughter Holly, was also in the play and he reckoned he had auditioned for the part. I knew this was bollocks, but pretending to take the bait, I went along with it. It was obviously a lie but with my brain now well and truly pickled, I blurted out how easy and simple it would be to do – a walk in the park, piece of cake. We're all actors, and well, I'd do it. Money was laid and bets were taken and beer was drunk.

I rang Karen.

"Are you being serious?" she demanded to know.

"Yep, sort me out an audition, " I replied.

As she was the leading lady playing Nancy, I knew she would have some clout. The Ormesby Players were a great bunch of people, and the production involved two stages, lights, an orchestra, kids, costumes, the full works. The kids playing the parts could only rehearse for so long due to some working laws, so basically there were two sets of them.

There were loads of people under 20 and quite a few past 50 and me in the middle. I got the part, but getting it was a real head fuck. One Sunday Karen picked me up for my audition and we went down to rehearsals. It was around teatime. I had had a few to drink for Dutch courage and was a bit pissed. Besides, I didn't want to let an audition spoil my Sunday session.

I had read through my lines for a few days, and it was just a case of saying them in context. I was introduced to everyone and the director (Gill), but they were under the cosh a bit working with the kids, so they asked me to go back at the end of rehearsals in a couple of hours.

No probs; cue nearest pub, that just happened to be over the road where I drank, drank, drank and read, read, read. Two hours later I was fluent at the part, but also very pissed. I staggered back in. I was in quite a state, with my script at the ready.

The four main characters looked at me.

"I want to do it on the stage, with the lights on and all of us in situ, " I told them.

I could easily become a diva, but they didn't seem to mind my excessive demands. Then it all went blurred. I remember a long pregnant pause and Gill looked at me with an expression I've never really seen before on a human being's face.

"Are you really that obnoxious and violent in real life?" she asked.

"Yes, pretty much so, what you see is what you get, " I told her.

"Okay, you've got the part then, " she said.

Olly would have been so proud of me. Monday morning. Fuck, fuck, fuckety fuck bad head; you know that feeling – you've done something wrong the night before and that it's only a matter of seconds before you work out what it was. But in those few seconds you're still innocent.

Then I remembered. I'd just committed myself to four months of rehearsals with old people and young kids and I'd have to slice big time into my annual leave to do it, but seeing my 20 missed calls and 30 texts, word had obviously got around. I had made my bed so now I had to lie in it. I was to become an actor and there was no going back.

To be fair it was fun, and I learnt a lot from those guys and even the kids. The old pros helped me immensely. I missed a few rehearsals though work and stuff (drink) but it was all coming together. The effort in putting on a show is immense. So many people were doing so much unseen work for nothing, but the love of it.

The play was running for four nights in September, and I had all summer to practise. Jue helped me a lot, reading through and playing other parts. In fact it got us into trouble one night on a campsite in France. Having been in a tent for a few days, the evenings would be spent running though my lines, with the boys playing, the sun shining and a few wines flowing. It was quite a laugh, but one night as we were rehearsing someone took offence.

One of my lines to Nancy (whose part Jue was reading for me) was: "You! Do you know what you are?"

"Yes, Bill, I know what I am and who I am, " read Jue.

"Well, shut your mouth or I'll shut it for a good long time to come, " I retorted, in character.

Right out of the blue this guy came racing over to the tent screaming merry hell, accusing me of abusing my wife and threatening to sort me out. We all had a laugh over it when I explained what was going on. The previous night, we'd rehearsed the scene where I killed Nancy with a carving knife, and she screamed the house down. If he'd been about then, God knows what might have happened.

On the opening night, and in true Coatesy style, I knew something was going to happen – it always does! The lads had rigged the hall with as many cameras as you see on a FA cup final day. There was a full blown OB (outside broadcast) The place was packed. All nights were sold out. There would be no hiding on this one. I was seriously nervous and had not slept for days. Could I really pull this off? I listened to all the advice, but was walking around like a zombie.

I have never been shy or embarrassed or slow at coming forward, but this was different. I didn't want to let myself down, but more importantly I didn't want to let anyone else down, and have people say great performance except for that twat who played Bill Sykes. Almost everyone I knew would be there. People were literally flying in to see me, so no pressure there then.

A few hours before curtains up, the boys and I were in Comet buying some tapes, even the lads wanted to take their own DV cameras to film me, despite the fact Spielberg and crew were in town. I walked past a very large plasma TV, there were quite a few people gathered round it, I took a look over to see what movie they were watching. A plane crashed into a tower block, then another, and the buildings collapsed. It was all on Sky News, my channel, which has appeared in movies before.

"Is this Independence Day 2 or something?" I asked.

"No, mate, that's the second twin tower that's just collapsed. The states are being attacked!"

"Yea right, " I said, and went to pay for the tapes.

Back at the car I put on the radio to hear: "And the second tower has now collapsed!"

Fucking hell, I was in shock. The only other time in my entire life I felt so shocked was when I got the call to say Diana had died. I don't know why, it was just a car crash. But here I was, curtains up in two hours and the whole world was being blown to pieces.

I turned to the boys and said: "This event is going to change the world pretty much as we know it – everything from flying, passports, travel, wars, conflicts, deaths, terrorism. Our lives will change because of what we're listening to now."

As news events go, they don't come much bigger. Turning up at the hall for my first performance, I was a bundle of nerves. Some had heard the news, but others, well they had more important things to think of. The play went ahead and got great reviews, despite one or two little problems like Mrs Bumble falling off Mr Bumble's knee and being admitted to A+E by ambulance, unconscious.

But all in all a great experience and as anyone who saw me will testify, I was fantastic, better even than the great Mr Reed himself. I was subsequently asked to play the Big Bad Wolf in the Christmas panto, but I had to turn it down, as I didn't want to be typecast, because he gets it in the end as well. The DVD of my performance is only a fiver!

Dive, Dive, Dive

We were sent to the Lake District to do a story about a small submarine that was to be used for showing tourists around the bottom of Lake Windermere. I love overnighting in the Lake District; the hotels are great and so is the food, but the scenery is really spectacular. I could happily retire there.

I know Windermere and the surrounding areas pretty well, having spent years water-skiing and boating over there, but I'd never been underneath it. The Dragons Den lads would have given this business idea pitch about three seconds before they threw it out.

Some guys had brought this 12-seat sub from the hot, clear and sealife-infested waters off the coast of Israel, to make a fortune sailing Jonny Tourist around the bottom of the lake in the summertime.

Trees, fences and wireless poles were chopped down to get it to its location. It was quite a sight to see this small sub on the back of a mighty low loader taking on the small country lanes of the Lake District. In fact as it trundled along the country lanes high above the hedges, it did, at some points, look as though it was sailing through the fields.

But the biggest drawback to their cunning plan was the fact that after 20-feet in Lake Windermere, all you can see is black, then some more black and then more black. It's a big deep cold barren lake with nothing to see except maybe a fish or two and that's on a good day. The remains of a long-lost civilization for sure is not down there, and even if it were, you wouldn't be able to see it.

Also, this thing, for whatever reason, can only go up and down, and not down and along as in most subs. We said a small prayer and jumped in. Sitting there in one of the 12 small seats, I was feeling a tad apprehensive. There were six people on board, or should I say souls – two pilots or drivers or whatever you call them, and two fare-paying passengers, and me and Tubb, the reporter.

Inside it was pretty much like a small plane, without a bar, or sick bags, but with a lot of windows. Not really for those of a claustrophobic disposition or indeed anyone that had had a lunchtime curry. I pointed the lens close to the glass so as not to get any reflections, and hit the record button.

Dive, dive, dive, the picture was quite cool, a lake on top, and water underneath the shot; David Attenborough stuff. We started to drop, now going green, now losing light, now black!

That's it, less than 10 seconds before we hit black out! Now what? I may have, just may have, got a shot of the tail of a fish, but the pictures would never stand up in a court of law. Drop, drop, drop, I think we were down 300 feet, but I could be wrong. Looking at the first two fare-paying passengers I got just a hint of disappointment. It did have lights, but even with them on, the visibility was down to two-feet. It really was pathetic. There could have been mermaids knocking at the windows and we wouldn't have seen them.

Our plan was to interview everyone at the bottom of the lake and do a piece to camera with Tubb saying: "Here we are at the bottom of Lake Windermere…"

Our daft sense of humour kicked in. Over the years we have done some shit stories but the powers that be have wanted them, and we are very good with silk purses and sows' ears and this job was right up there with the worst of them.

The drop took a while and Tubb reckoned he'd just seen Atlantis, and I was pretty sure out the starboard window I saw Donald Campbell, but having pointed out to me, he bought it on Coniston Water, so it must have been someone else.

As we got to the bottom the engines stopped. We did chats with the tourists, who surprisingly said it was a waste of money; then chats with the owner drivers who said it was the best thing ever to happen on the lake. Then Tubb did his piece to camera: "Here we are on the bottom of the lake."

Thinking about it we were on the bottom for some time. When I say bottom, it's not like being in your local swimming pool with concrete and tiles. The bottom of the lake is silt, thick gooey silt, thousands of years old and hundreds of meters thick.

Unbeknown to us, as we sat there, we were gradually being sucked into it more and more, and deeper and deeper, like being sucked into a blancmange that's made of superglue. Once we'd finished filming and all was done, we were ready to surface.

"Up we go, " I said. "We're finished. Let's get out of here!"

Nothing, no movement, no nothing. It was obvious the engines was straining. They sounded hurt. The boss man explained we were stuck in the silt, no worries. No worries, no fucking worries, panic had set in all around.

It all went slow mo as again and again he tried to rock us free. Up and down, back and front, stopping and starting the engines, for what send like an eternity.

I remembered an old airline pilot joke and the pilot says: "We're in a bit of trouble but if you repeat after me things should be all right. Our father, who art in heaven…"

No one spoke but the atmosphere was intense. Beads of sweat were dropping from my forehead and icy cold sweat dripped down my back. I started to think about recording my own obituary and the subsequent news reports when our bodies were recovered and the tape played out on TV.

Would Sky give it to other news outlets or would they run it exclusively? Watch tonight live and see one of our crews and reporter die in front of you. Some viewers my find this distressing…That always get the viewing figures up.

It's amazing what goes through your head at the prospect of death. But then pop, like a champagne cork, we took off upwards. I really, to this day, don't know how close we were from a watery grave.I know that the sub had 12 hours of air on board, but stuck 300 feet down in the shit on the bottom of Windermere, I'm not too sure who would have got us out. I have great dreams over this incident, or are they called coffin nightmares?

Lady Di

I have filmed the Royals many times over the years. In fact I think I have done them all, from the Queen, Prince Philip, Charles, the late Queen Mother and most of their sons and daughters, but never, for some reason, the boys, William and Harry.

I even spoke to their mother Princess Di on a few occasions. In fact, I was there the day Dennis Pollet, a Manchester cameraman for us, got those amazing pictures of Diana getting into a car and bursting into tears. The pics went global. It was really the first indication that her marriage was on the rocks. It came on the back of some trip she and Charles had just come back from and apparently they didn't want to be together. It was the beginning of the end of a real life fairy story. Really quite sad.

We sometimes forgot that not only was she a princess, but also a person, mother and wife. The media tended to forget the last bit most of the time, and treated her as a walking news story, making headlines wherever she went. She was indeed the most famous person in the world, and she played the game, but hey, being chased to your death by a pack of preying paps was well over the pale.

Despite all the conspiracy theories, I believe the media pretty much killed her and we were all tarred with the same brush. It didn't help that her driver that night was pissed and high, but the industry really did have to stand back and take a good look at themselves. We did, but after a few months everyone was back to their old tricks, phone tapping, stalking the hotels and nightspots, sitting outside houses and living in bushes. The public demanded it.

The other times I filmed her, she didn't come across as you see on TV, with all the attributes and stunning looks. To me she always looked worried and stressed. No doubt she knew how to make people feel relaxed and special and she really did have an aura about her, but she was so complex I doubt very much anyone actually knew the real Diana, even her ex-husband.

One time she was a bit pissed off at me for sticking a camera in her face most of the afternoon, and as she got back in the car, she looked out of the window straight into my eyes, and put her tongue out. I didn't know whether to laugh or cry, so I just smiled and nodded, as if to say: "Look, I'm really sorry, but I'm just doing my job. Actually I hate pissing people off, or imposing on someone's grief." It just seems wrong and I wouldn't want hordes of media sitting on my doorstep if I was in mourning. Anyway, she can't have meant it.

Prince Charles once rode over my foot on a bicycle that had been designed for disabled people. The handlebars were underneath the seat, and he was giving it whirl, much to the delight of the inventors, who subsequently when on to make fuck all, as it was the world's worst-designed bike for disabled people ever built.

He rode towards me, out of control. His security people grabbed me to get out of the way, another got hold of the other cameraman, but they didn't realise there was an umbilical cable between us, and as they pulled and pushed nothing happened. The wall behind us didn't help matters either. He just skimmed my toe, and as I was about to go down like Klinsmann (German footballer known for diving), he apologised, saying: "I'm sorry, young man!"

I didn't hear the rest because of the security men bollocking me for not getting out of the way!

The late Queen Mum was always great to be around. Covering her visits was a very relaxed affair. There was no running or jumping about or racing to the next photo call. Even the snappers became subdued whenever she was in town. Always smiling, it would be hard for anyone not to warm to her. She was your favourite gran, and seemed genuinely interested in everyone she met and what was being said.

As a little girl, she knew the Bowes Museum in Barnard Castle very well – it was linked to her family, the Bowes-Lyons. I am sure one of her favourite things was seeing the museum's prize possession, a very old silver swan, pluck a fish out of a river. This wasn't just any old swan. This was 100 odd years old, fully-sized, solid silver and had moving mechanics that had not been touched since the day it was made. It gets wound up a few times a year. A truly beautiful thing.

On one visit to the museum, I remember the look on her face as it started moving, and playing its tune. The joy that came out of that old lady's face was truly amazing, I think it really must have touched a cord and brought back a lot of good memories from days in her youth.

Golf

The cold night air sent shivers running down my spine. The car door slammed with a mighty bang as I got out. It was all very still and subdued. The music from the radio still repeated lyrics in my head. As I looked around, more cars arrived, stopped and became silent, headlights dying in the dark.

The salty taste of sea air danced on the tongue, a low chatter erupted, and slowly as the eyes adapted, it became apparent that the dead of night had gone but the figures in the distant made no sense as yet.

A friendly face appeared with a sarcastic quip.

"So you couldn't sleep either?"

Owen, a snapper from Press Association, and old sparring partner, smiled and opened his car boot, the courtesy light illuminated a bright shiny array of golf clubs. Five o'clock in the morning is really not the greatest time in the day to practise your swing or indeed chipping, but being early on a job sometimes does have its advantages. Besides there's not much else to do in a shipyard at daybreak in Barrow.

Whacking a few balls into the dock seemed like a good idea at the time. A 9 iron and a mighty perfect swing, sorry imperfect swing, set the blood moving, and as the balls disappeared into the void it was just possible to make out in the distance the shape of a large, very large silhouetted object.

Slowly it became a bit more visible, a Trident nuclear submarine. We teed up our balls and drove for the conning tower. There was this hollow tinning noise as I scored my first nuke in one, followed shortly after by a very intense searchlight, and two pairs of security feet. With howls of laughter we ran and hid like little kids. Mind it did make some noise in the stillness of the night.

I do apologise to Her Majesty's Navy for leaving a small dent on their seriously expensive piece of kit, but safe to say it will never happen again. The shot was an absolute fluke.

The War

"What did you do in the war, Daddy?"

"Well, Son, let me tell you. I ate vast amounts of pasta and drank copious amounts of red wine!"

I have had the opportunity to cover several war zones, the most recent being Afghanistan. Sky wanted to send someone into Afghanistan with the troops to look for Bin Laden, who they thought was holing up in the Tora Bora Mountains. It would involve a three-month trip high up in the mountains, during winter, and living as the lads do. All they wanted were pictures of either Bin Laden's death or capture (yea right).

I was told due to the onset of winter the trip might be longer. It seemed a bit of a no brainier to me. Call me old-fashioned, but I have a bit of an aversion to bombs and bullets, indeed even to death. Besides, the new football season was just kicking off. So I said thanks, but no thanks. Again I said no thanks when we were all asked who would like to cover the last Gulf War.

I knew, from experience, if I said yes I would have no choice where I went. I could end up covering the war from the top of a five-star hotel in some bizarre Middle East country, or on the other hand, I could end up embedded with a highly-strung US marine unit, just spoiling for a fight.

As I am a betting man and have never won the Lotto or indeed even a bottle of Advocaat at the school fete, I had a good idea where

I might end up, so once again, I said thanks but no thanks. I really didn't want to experience war and have those memories with me for the rest of my life. It wasn't for me.

I know a few guys that get off on that sort of stuff and let me assure you it screws your brain. People who cover those sorts of conflicts do so for many reasons, mainly the experience, but for sure it's about finding and pushing yourself, coping under fire, living off the basics and being able to function both as a human being and also actually working in that environment, with the real prospect of death being just around the corner.

I admire their bravery and professionalism, but it's really not for me, but the story must be told, so someone has to do it. I wish them all safe travels.

I have only once been to a war zone – Kosovo, the conflict that no one understood, unless of course you lived there. It was complicated and messy, and we went down to cover it, from the safety of an air base in Italy. We were based near an airfield in a place in southern Italy.

The RAF had a big presence there and were flying sorties with GR7s (harriers to you and me).

They left after breakfast and came home after a bit of bombing for lunch. We were the pool crew. In extreme circumstances the media will share resources so everyone has access to everyone else's pictures. It works most of the time. It certainly makes sense both financially and physically to have as few people as possible in dangerous situations and the news media co-operate well in this sort of situation.

Once the lads were safely back from doing their bit, it was great. We had pasta, pizza and red wine. It's amazing really but food in southern Italy contains very little garlic, if at all, so my palate had to adapt.

We were there to make sure that the fly boys really did make it back in one piece, otherwise we would have a news story on our hands, with downed aircraft and missing air crew. Fortunately all went well and the only sorties that were missed were by pilots spraining and twisting ankles whilst playing five-a-side, to the degree that the medical officer stopped all play, because too many injuries were screwing up the war a bit.

Blair at the time demanded "a zero body count" for air crew, which meant nothing dangerous. This meant bombing from a safe distance, about 15, 000 feet, well out of the range of and SAMs (surface to air missiles). A lot of bombs never hit their targets so civilians' lives could have been lost because the RAF usually drop bombs from about 500 feet and do so very effectively, but they had never trained to release them from so high up. This was a bit of a fuck up, but we broke the story, and were subsequently hated by the RAF.

The squadron leader told me that evening that Gerard Tubb (our reporter), was a twat, wanker, cunt, anti-army, air force, and navy, and not patriotic enough. He then went on to have a bit of a rant. Tubbs decided to stay away from the bar that night as he knew he may well have been hanged so I took the flak on behalf of Sky News with a "thank you Squadron Leader, I'll make sure I pass it on."

After a few weeks it did get a bit boring until one day whilst filming round the air base we were arrested at gun point. The set up was that the air base belonged to the Italians, and was guarded by them with rapier missiles and such like, but was used by the Brits with their Harriers and by the Americans with an assortment of aircraft, the most prominent being the A10, also known as the warthog, an amazing plane. As a plane spotter I could go on, but I won't.

We were spending a day with our chums from across the pond,

being given big PR licks by them. We were looking over their aircraft and talking to the lads, when we strayed somewhere we shouldn't have, whilst being escorted by our American officers, who basically had no idea what was in and out of limits. All hell broke loose.

The Italian guards took us and the Americans and whoever else was within 100 yards, at gunpoint to see the headmaster, or whatever rank he was. He was not amused. We, of course, for once, were completely innocent (the first and only time). Words were said, and apologies were given and we went on our way, with the Yanks eating big chunks of humble pie.

The air base is massive and you need a car or bike to get around. The focus point for the Americans is the cappuccino bar, a big fucking coffee shop right, in the middle of the airfield. It's better than Starbucks. While we heard stories about the Brits not having any money for stationery, the Americans really did bring all the home comforts with them and wanted for nothing, Government take note! A big sign we passed read "we feed the hog". It was the ammunition lads' little joke and I am sure I could smell weed going past it. Another thing the Yanks like doing is parking all their planes together, which make quite an impressive sight. But as one British officer pointed out, one lucky air strike could take them all out, whereas we parked ours a long way apart and hid them under a tarpaulin. He had a point!

The only other day of note was the day I nearly died, twice. The Armed Forces Minister arrived at the airbase and we were tasked with covering his visit and making sure he was seen to be doing his job and jollying up the troops. Everything was very hush hush and we had no idea of the plans. We just knew we could be going into theatre; that is to say, into the actual war zone.

Things were on a need-to-know basis and we were told fuck all. We flew out of the air base in two Sea King helicopters, and after several hours we landed in the dark, in a war zone on board HMS Illustrious, one of our few aircraft carriers.

I have no idea how, in the pitch darkness, with all lights off, these guys manage such flying. It's beyond me. After we landed we went on deck to film some returning Harriers, when a plane was coming back after a mission. Known as recovering an aircraft, these guys were landing their aeroplanes, in darkness on board a completely blacked-out ship, in the middle of the sea on an unbalanced platform, with cross winds, in a war zone.

The Harrier is one of the few planes in the world that can actually hover. Looking down the view finder I could see nothing, yet it was only metres away. You had to wear ear protectors because your ears would explode due to the screaming jet engines. It was a feat of flying only a few of our top gun pilots can actually achieve.

"Yes Captain, all very impressive, " we thought, "but how's about drinky poos in your cabin?" We actually went to the boardroom. The Captain of the Illustrious and all the other Captains of the other relevant ships in the battle group were there along with the Minister, and the Admiral of the Fleet, Sir Someone Or Other, who knew fuck all about football.

Canapes and chit chat amongst the most powerful men afloat, covered in so much gold braid you could not tell there was a blue jacket underneath. It was right up my street, I was right at home! It wasn't a case of "Please, for fuck's sake, someone ask me what football team I support, or at least what the weather is going to be like tomorrow!"

We were introduced to everyone, and we got into conversation with the Admiral and the Armed Forces Minister, who were being told by an aide what the plan was. "You'd better let me in on this one, lads, cos I'm taking the pictures, " I mentioned.

So I was told the cunning plan. We were to spend the night on board, and then at first light we were to fly by helicopter to our nuclear submarine HMS Splendid, where the Armed Forces Minister was to be lowered down from the chopper by hoist and into the sub, which was somewhere off Malta.

"A wise and cunning plan, " I explained to the Admiral. "Except to get the best pictures of the Minister being lowered onto the sub, I would actually have to be in another helicopter as it was almost impossible to shoot vertically down from one, as experience has taught me.

A short pause later, and now one of my favourite sayings, the Admiral turned to the ship's Captain and said, "Get this man a helicopter!" How cool was that? And indeed they did. I also wanted a well-stocked bar on board and two pretty trolly dollies as well.

Having spent a few hours trying to sleep on some board in a storeroom, eventually sleeping on the floor, I was awoken just before first light and taken to a small canteen area and given coffee and the obligatory bacon sandwich. I gave the egg a miss, and was introduced to my crew.

I can only remember the name of the pilot, Stu, who had no idea who the fuck I was, and why he was flying on his day off. He was a tad pissed off, but we took off in his Lynx helicopter anyway and followed the Sea King that the Minister was in. He really had no idea where we were going.

In a helicopter the pilot sits in the right seat and the co-pilot the left, opposite to a fixed wing aircraft. I was sitting in the back by myself with headphones and intercom on, and we soon struck up a bit of rapport. After a few hours we'd covered the important subjects of football and drinking. I, on the other hand, found it fascinating and wanted to know all about the aircraft, its weapon systems, how long they had been flying and all the other stuff.

One thing that really starting to interest me was how long could this bird fly for. Stu reckoned about four hours give or take a bit. Now my Maths aren't great, but hadn't we already been flying for nearly two and a half hours? Even with things going smoothly and getting shots of the Minister being winched down on to the sub, we would be in the air for maybe over five hours. I didn't want to sound like a twat, but I was curious to know, how did we get back?

Stu told me not to fret, there were plenty of our ships in the area to land and refuel on.

"We do it every day, " he told me.

On a turquoise blue sea a large menacing shape appeared. It was HMS Splendid and did she look splendid? We dropped down to 50 feet and got some great pictures of the Minister being lowered by winch from the Sea King on to the sub. After 20 minutes or so the transaction was complete and we headed for home. The Lynx is one of the fastest helicopters flying and we were flat out on the way back. With the lack of fuel still being a bit of an issue to me, Stu spotted a pod of dolphins.

"Do you want to take a look?" he asked.

There I was, at sea in a war zone, flying at zero feet, over a pod of jumping dolphins, and it was one of the most exhilarating experiences I have ever had. It was just mind-blowing!

There was a bing sound in the headphones. It was the fuel warning light coming on, and just as in a car, the fuel gauge was on red. It was time to refuel. No problem, let's pop down somewhere and get some gas.

A French aircraft carrier was just over the horizon so we

thought we'd get down there for a couple of gallons. No, we wouldn't, it would be a problem, we were told; she was recovering aircraft.

Stu reckoned it still wasn't a problem. HMS Grafton was just up the road. No problem, she'll sort us out. As she came into view I was a tad relieved. Once on deck, three cups of tea were presented to us as we asked for 50 litres of leaded please.

Except there was a problem. Now I can't believe that this problem was not sorted out before anyone went to war and made sure everything worked, but the nozzle of the fuel pipe onboard the Grafton did not fit in the spout of the Lynx's fuel tank. That's is what I was led to believe, so we still couldn't refuel. Still not a problem, for even further up the road was HMS Coventry. For sure they would be able to sort out our little problem.

Up again we went. By now there was some anxiety in the air, and there were those bloody "Bing Bing" sounds again. I was starting to shit myself a bit now and asked: "How far, Stu?"

Not long, he told me, then we heard bing bing again. I knew this wasn't good. Then there was a Bong" and another "Bong" and an alarm that wasn't the fuel warning sound rang out.

"God, this is it. We're going to ditch!" I thought.

Having seen what happens when choppers hit the water, I knew I would be lucky to come out alive. But the situation was even worse than I had imagined.

Stu screamed: "We've just been locked onto."

My headset was unplugged and all hell broke loose. Again. Apparently after we left Grafton and headed for the Coventry nobody had told the Coventry that we were coming, the lads thought the Grafton had told her and the Grafton had thought we had told her. So there we were, incoming fast and low, and unidentified and heading straight for a Navy ship in a combat zone. Well, what would you think!

I was eventually put back in the picture, and just had visions of a large bright missile flying into the side of us and disappearing beneath the waves.

It didn't happen. We landed, refuelled and headed back to the Illustrious. It was a silent ride back to the ship. Not much was said. I still can't believe I thanked Stu and his navigator for the trip.

The Boro

One story that Gazza wasn't involved in is that of Paul Merson leaving Middlesbrough to join Aston Villa. I know one tale of why Gazza had made his teammate Mers leave the Boro was certainly untrue, because I made it up.

I have been a Boro supporter and season ticket holder for many years. I get to most of the home games with the boys and have watched them both at Ayresome Park and the Riverside Stadium since I was about ten. I have seen them in all the Wembley finals and indeed the final of UEFA Cup in Eindhoven, not to mention the time when we won our first, and at this rate probably last, bit of silverware at the Millenium Stadium in Cardiff.

As with all Boro trips, there is a story and the further the trip, the better the story. The press conference involving Merson's departure to the Villa is worth telling.

Paul Merson, a very good footballer in his day, was leaving the Boro to join Villa. Mers had had a few off-the-field problems to say the least – drink, drugs, gambling. He was just your everyday Premiership footballer really.

Boro held a press conference to confirm his departure and I turned up with a freelance reporter who shall remain anonymous. He was a bit green, and certainly no footie correspondent. The lads were there, and my brother Jon, who was working for the local BBC. We were all early and having a bit of crack {not the drug} about who's doing what to who, what you've been doing, and speculating why Mers had left the Boro.

As a local guy that sort of held a few ins and outs at the club, it fell on me to give the definitive answer.

The London reporter I was with seemed to think I was the chairman's right hand man, so I didn't let him down.

"Come on Coatesy, what's the story here then?" he asked me.

Looking at our lad with a twinkle in his eye, we just made up the first thing that came into our heads.

"Well, you see it's like this, " we started.

We "revealed" Mers was having a few problems staying off the booze and keeping out of the bookies, and every morning after training, coming out the shower, he was opening his kit bag to reveal cans of Kestrel Super Strength Lager and playing cards, not to mention bookies betting slips. Gazza was the one who'd been putting them there, we claimed. Mers had got so pissed off with it all that he was leaving.

The London reporter looked at us both with that "you really do have the inside track" look and took in every word. To be fair, with hindsight it really is the sort of thing Gazza would have done.

Our man was now ready for the press conference. Me and our lad really couldn't believe he'd taken in any of the bollocks we had just spouted to him. Sitting on the table was the Boro's then manager Bryan Robson and next to him was chief exec Keith three points Lamb (in joke).

With the two teams assembled, the media and them, the conference went ahead with some pretty boring mundane stuff – comments about "good move for both parties", "best wishes" and "great servant to the club".

They made all the right noises but they didn't reveal the real reason why he was leaving. As in politics, they just glossed over everything and told us what they wanted to.

The press conference was nearing the end with Lamb asking: "Any more questions?"

There was silence. That's it, I thought, it was lunchtime. But before I could take the camera off the tripod, a voice in the background (the London reporter) was asking one last fact-finding question.

"Mr Robson, is there any truth in the rumour that Merson left because Gazza was putting cans of super strength lager in his wash bag?"

Now that question wouldn't have been out of place in a news conference with news reporters; no one would have batted an eyelid. But with the football hacks and sports journalists, who have to cover the club almost every day and lick the boots of everyone associated with it, it was akin to asking whether Mrs Robson took it up the arse! You just don't do it. You may think it, or debate it with your mates, but you just don't ask it! Well, he just had!

May I just point out at this stage that a 6 foot 15-stone cameraman can actually disappear into a 2cm by 2cm viewfinder! Jon looked at me. I looked at him. I just could not believe what he just said.

I was biting down hard on my tongue to stop laughing. Here we go! Robson looked at him as though he had just taken the lives of his family. Lamb did too. He also looked pretty amazed.

After a long pause Robson said, "Are you trying to be funny with me, son?"

Lamb was whispering in Robson's ear just off-mic: "Who is this fucking joker? Where the fuck's security? Get this cunt out of here!"

Big burly men were scurrying towards the London reporter

who repeated: "Mr Robson, I am not trying to be funny, I want to know if there's any truth in this rumour."

It was great. We didn't realise he had actually taken our little josh as gospel. He wouldn't let it lie. Top marks to the lad. As his little feet flapped above the ground and his vertical body was flying though the door, all you could hear was: "I asked a perfectly straightforward question, Mr Robson, and I demand an answer."

It wasn't the first time we were thrown out of a football club and banned, but hey, it goes with the territory.

About six months later a friend of ours Jen, who lives in Brighton and gets back for a couple of games a season, was saying she knew why Mers had left the Boro. It was all down to Gazza putting cans of super strength lager in his change bag.

"Where did you hear that from, Jen?" we asked.

"A bloke down our local told me!" she revealed.

Her local was in Brighton! Our story had made the south coast! All the way from Middlesbrough!

Never believe what you read or hear! Especially when it comes to football matters!

The Black Hole

Boulby Mine, I believe, is the deepest mine in Europe. When not mining for potash used in the fertilizer industry, they mine for rock salt, the stuff we put on the roads when it's icy. Someone somewhere down at Sky thought it would be a good idea to see this process from start to finish, God knows why.

The mine is on the North East coast between Whitby and Middlesbrough and I have covered stories there many times before, but I've never been down it. We got changed into our mining gear – overalls, steel toe capped boots and hard hats with lights – and headed to the lift shaft with our escort.

The lift is a sort of double lift with one cage above another, and maybe 18 or more men in each. The cage doors closed and we started our descent, slowly at first, then whoosh, we were in frigging free fall, with little light in the cage and a feeling of weightlessness. I started flapping. Fucking hell, the cable's snapped! I thought. We're all going to die.

Looking around for some reassurance, I caught the eye of some big hairy-arsed miner, who looked at me and asked, "Did you see Match of the Day at the weekend?"

Panic over, this feeling of plummeting to certain death is normal, and these guys do it every day, so yes I put on a this-doesn't-scare-me-face and replied, "The Boro where truly shit and Man U were lucky again."

My kids would pay a small fortune for a ride like that, and I got it for free. Now I guess most people think a mine is small, cramped and compacted and you walk crouched down with a torch in your helmet flickering everywhere. Well, this place was lit up like Bonfire Night. When you get to the bottom of the shaft you have to walk to a bus stop. The buses, to be fair, are not double deckers but trannie vans with the van bit removed and seats all over the back.

We jumped on one, heading for the pit face. It was a 25-minute ride blasting through massive tunnels in the pitch black and somewhere near the earth's core. We slowed down at one point for someone to point out a sign on the roof that read. You are now under the North Sea – very comforting!

We arrived at the face where the lads were mining and started filming. The machine that gets the salt out is a sort of massive round blade with a conveyor belt coming out – not too dissimilar to those pictures you see when the Channel Tunnel was dug. It was a similar type of rock-eating monster.

We all stood round and one of the guys explained what was going to happen when the machine started drilling. We should stand here and this and that's going to happen and so on. Oaky dokey, no problem there then.

As I looked round I could see none of the lads were wearing their face masks. Mine was hanging around my neck, and, wanting to be cool and look hard like the rest of them, I kept it there. What a mistake that was. The machine started up and a wall of salt came hurtling towards me. Within seconds, I was covered in it from head to foot.

I must have had my mouth open because all I remember is chewing on the stuff, eating a large mouthful of salt is no fun; so much salt, in fact, that I started wretching and throwing up five miles under the North Sea, much to the delight and amusement of all the miners. I'll do anything for a laugh! We finished shooting and returned to the surface. You have no idea what clean fresh air tastes like after that.

I have every admiration for people who work in those conditions. In fact, conditions down there are so corrosive due to the salt that you have to wrap the camera up in clingfilm or it will literally start rusting in front of your eyes. Salt and electrics just do not go.

I must have missed a bit as a few days later the zoom on my lens started to make a sound like an elephant giving birth every time I used it. I think I may well have totalled it from going down there.

On a plus point, from that day onwards, I have never been able to have salt on any of my food; the smell and the taste still makes me wretch. Yes, I am the one that eats my chips salt-less. In fact I have just invented a remedy for people who are salt-dependent – take a trip down Boulby!

The news piece that went out was indeed **Bafta** material – all my pieces are! Here is a mine; here is the salt being mined in the mine; there is a cameraman being sick, (surprisingly not through alcohol); here is a train that takes the salt from the mine to the depot; this is the truck that puts the salt on the road when it's icy, gripping stuff indeed.(no pun intended).

You should have seen the look on the mine manager's face when we told him our news editor would refuse to run the story if it wasn't the exact salt that was mined earlier in the day coming out the back of the gritting lorry. I even think he started to make phone calls.

So now you know where salt comes from, but you can't put it on your chips as it's rock salt, but if you're daft enough, you can just eat it raw!

The Blair Years

Politics. Oh dear where do you begin?

Writing this during the expenses row and my heart just bleeds for them! I hope the robbing bastards get a little taste of porridge. I have never been a political animal. The only party I would ever vote for is the popular people's front of Judea, and definitely not the people's popular front of Judea, splitters.

I like Blair, as a person he has everything you would wish for in a Prime Minister. He wasn't an embarrassment like Brown or Bush on the world stage. I mean, who else could play head tennis with a football with Kevin Keegan? Impressive.

His politics and the few little wars he started will be judged by historians in the years to come, but with regards to his presence in front of a camera, it has to be said he was good.

After the death of John Smith, Labour flung all their eggs into one basket with Blair, gave him the Sedgefield constituency and bided their time till he became the PM, which he duly did.

However, Sedgefield is only 15 minutes up the road from where I live, so needless to say every time he came back up to his constituency, which normally was the last Friday in every month, I was there to greet him... and all his personal protection chums, and special branch and CID and the local bobbies.

And when visiting Heads of State came to town with all their chums like Jacques Chirac or the boy Bush or whoever, then the fun just never stopped. All us media types had just a great time, trying to do our jobs and not listening to those Labour Party paranoid control freaks, who even had the audacity to ask to look down my view finder to check Blair would look his best.

In the early years, even before Blair was the head of the Labour Party, things were a bit more relaxed. Most Fridays or Saturday mornings I would stand at the end of his drive and get shots of him going backwards and forwards to Teesside Airport to catch flights to London.

There was a change in the air and most political analysts would have taken a large punt on Blair being the next PM, so it was time to start recording his life in some detail. His campaign manager in Sedgefield was a really nice guy called John Burton, who I got on really well with over the years.

In my opinion John's downfall at the time was his passion for Sunderland FC, and with me being a big Boro boy, he endured many years of piss-take. How things have changed. Am glad I don't see him now as he'd have my life!

One morning, standing in the cold and pouring rain by myself, John came out. This is the kind of guy he was. He said: "Look, this is silly. Come into the house, make yourself a cup of tea in the kitchen and I'll give you the heads-up before he leaves."

Cheers John!

Another time I was sitting in Blair's kitchen waiting for him to do a turn, and I was with my reporter, and we were having a browse though Cherie's cookbooks, as you do. Or were they Tony's? Probably not, but there did seem to be a lot of hand-written recipes for pies. We love pies up North so I guess they'd thought when in Rome...

Shooting someone so regularly over so many years, it was

interesting to see the physical changes in him. The stresses and strains of being the PM have obviously taken their toll and I'm sure the bloke has aged beyond his years. No wonder he has a dicky ticker.

But he is loved by everyone in the Sedgefield area – I suspect because of his personality. He has certainly visited every school, business, hospital and old folks' home in the area, and to be fair he has done a great deal for the people up here. There doesn't seem to be any red tape or lack of funding in Sedgefield.

But now he's out to grass, trying to sort out the Middle East or something. It's certainly a lot less stressful then being one of the most well-known world leaders.

In fact his number two, big bad Prescott was also on my patch and I have a few stories about him, but I won't tell them due to the fact I know he'll come up and punch my lights out!

The only time I have ever really panicked or got stressed out in front of so-called personalities was in front of Prescott and his wife Pauline. I was doing an interview with them in a hotel in Durham, when halfway though the chat, I could smell burning.

John pointed out that one of my lights was on fire. I turned around only to realize that the plug on one of my lights was indeed on fire and hot burning plastic had set the carpet alight in one of their fine suites.

I put it out and did the honourable thing by pushing a large table over the big blackened hole I'd made in their luxurious carpet – after I'd opened all the windows! We just carried on as though nothing had happened and you can't prove anything!

Another of Tony's cronies is my mate Mandy. At one point he was even coming along to see a play I was in, but fortunately he didn't show.

My brother Jon who, as you know, is a cameraman for the local BBC up here will hate me for telling this story but it's all in the best possible taste.

Jon's patch is mainly in the Teesside area, which of course includes Hartlepool, Mandelson's constituency. Mandy was also in the cabinet as minister without portfolio. At the time regular as clockwork Jon would turn up at Mandy's house to interview him about the local issues. Over time Jon was becoming more and more reluctant to turn up, even trying to get other crews to do the job for him.

One night talking shop over a few beers and been heavily pressed by me he came out with it. Mandy fancied him! The table just exploded with laughter! Jon's embarrassment was and still is just unimaginable, but I said: "Jon, you're a good-looking guy. Why wouldn't he fancy you?"

You can imaging the shit he got. I have no reason to doubt him. It's not like he's been in TV for as long as me and knows what's what!

But the consensus of opinion was despite the fact he has a wife and two kids is that he should give it a try! You never know! If you know Jon, you must never ask him about it, it's our little secret!

Personally I don't give a shit what anyone's sexual persuasion is in life, but what I do find amazing is that someone in office screws up so badly that he gets kicked out into the wilderness, hangs around lying low for a while and comes back as Lord Mandelson of Hartlepool and FOE. Am I missing something?

Blair, as we found out to our cost, hates surprises. One sunny Friday afternoon covering a Blair visit, his people asked us if we were going back to his constituency house that afternoon. It was his birthday and a big surprise party had been planned. Of course we were up for anything that involved free booze and food.

Now, hand on heart, I cannot remember who was to blame for spoiling his big day, either my reporter or his people, but somewhere along the line, someone screwed up. For a change it wasn't me.

We had just finished doing a chat with Blair about whatever relevant subject the newsdesk wanted us to ask him about, and exchanging a few niceties after the interview when the reporter said: "See you this afternoon then."

Blair looked a him puzzled and replied something along the lines of: "I think not, the rest of the day is private. You've had your cents worth, now leave me alone."

Blair pressed him further until it was revealed that we were all meeting up round his place to celebrate his birthday, with a glass of wine and a chunk of cake. Blair lost the plot, and blew up at some junior lackey. Did you know about this?

In turn he asked everyone if they knew about this. Everyone nodded or said yes. He blew his stack and wandered off bellowing about how much he hated surprises, and whose fucking idea was this, and a whole bunch of other stuff. He wasn't a happy bunny.

Sure enough we all piled round Blair's pad and drank his wine and ate his cake. Some of the lads have a reputation for being buffet slayers, so a bit of advice if you ever put on a spread and the media are in tow, make sure they eat last, or there will be tears.

Blair did his birthday speech and started off by thanking my reporter and Sky News for fucking up his birthday surprise and chuntered on about how nice it all was, and a hearty thank you for all coming and making the effort to see me, and what a lovely surprise it was. The lying bastard.

Crashes

These days I never fly on an aircraft unless there's a bar on board. Anything that's too small to have a bar on board in my opinion is just far too dangerous.

I have seen many accidents over the years – bus, trains, cars, even ship crashes (that doesn't sound right), but some of the stuff I've seen still gives me nightmares. It's part of the job, and a part I really hate. You never really come to terms with black bags and grieving relatives. When I get back home and the wife and kids ask: "How's your day been, Daddy?" I just lie. These days I seem to lie a lot. There's no good news, remember!

Small aircraft are fundamentally dangerous, so are military fast jets. They are forever coming down all over the bloody place. Check out Ceefax mid June and July. Every other page seems to have tales of small planes crashing all over the country and busting into flames or just missing some village or other.

Helicopters for me are just a big no no. Far too many people die in them – mostly celebs or very rich people. Do not ever get in one.

In my dumbass youth I'd jump into anything that took to the sky, without giving it a second thought. When a hotel fell off a cliff and into the sea at Scarborough, I was the mug that got into someone's kit helicopter and buzzed about getting pictures for all and sundry. Being piston-driven, it couldn't even hover. When the

North Sea breeze hits those cliffs, the air flow just goes vertical and so do you. The chopper pilots that check out pylons are just plum crazy. Much of what I shot that day over the stricken hotel was unusable due to the fact I had my eyes shut.

I once had to jump into the back of a Chinook at very short notice, so short in fact that I wasn't given ear plugs or a headset. I was told to put my fingers in my ears. No problem there then when you're operating a camera! When I took my fingers out to film, the pain in my ears was so bad due to the noise I just gave up taking any pictures.

We did a story on a businessman who used his private jet to do business all over Europe and still be back home for tea at the end of the day. We flew to Denmark for the afternoon and then to Manchester. From Manchester we flew to Newcastle – a journey that took 19 minutes. We had a loss of power on take-off and instead of the nose pointing up it was pointing down, not a great feeling.

And once coming back from covering the Balkans War, we were about to land at Amsterdam Airport when we had to do an emergency go around. I have never seen so many people crying and praying, me included. I never did find out what had happened. Someone said there was a plane still on the runway. I do know our pilot that day was a young good-looking blonde pony-tailed girl, who got us down safely.

We used to have an office at Teesside Airport right next door to the flying school and at weekends the instructors would only be too happy to take you up with their pupils in return for a couple of beers in the bar afterwards.

The old stall manoeuvre is a great one for the faint-hearted. Get up a couple of thousand feet and switch the engine off. The trick then is to try to get it going again before you hurtle to your death at unimaginable speed. These little four seat Pipers or Cessnas simply do not glide – they fucking plummet – and it always seemed to take far too long in my book to get that engine going again! So I knocked that on the head.

My hat goes off to all those lads that work offshore. No wonder they get paid so much, but they deserve every penny. There was a large loss of life in Morecambe Bay the other year when a chopper came down – a story we covered.

Getting on and off the platforms in the North Sea has seen many accidents over the years. It's bloody dangerous.

Lockerbie happened on a Wednesday night. We went up a few days later, and most of the place was cordoned off. The village was in deep shock and when I went back for a remembrance service and anniversary recently, the place still is in shock. It will take a whole generation to get over what happened that night, and everyone living there is still affected in some way.

The RAF put on a decent crash though, mainly at sea and fortunately normally without loss of life. We should all be given ejector seats and parachutes. The lads also like to practise over the wilds of Northumberland and the Lake District. The pilots that crashed their jet into the centre of the small village of Shap were branded heroes, and in my view anyone who puts their lives at risk with the aim of protecting our country is a hero. But they both died. I'm sure the scenario could have been worse, but for their heroism.

However, you do sometimes wonder what weaponry is on board. A few years ago there were big European war manoeuvres over the Scottish Borders with Air Forces practising dog fighting and war games. I kid you not. They were coming down like rain, at least three in as many weeks.

The newsdesk was flapping. An air crash is big news and we

went to the first two. Most of the time there's not much to see, mostly some mangled bits of steel and burnt heather. After a few weeks we gave up covering them. In fact it became so common I think we even gave up reporting on them. It became: "Another tornado down, pilots ejected safely and now the weather."

I even remember the wife saying, "Not another one." My sister-in-law lives on the south coast and has one of those little huts on the beach at Calshot. She phoned one night a tad upset because a tornado had hit the beach and she was unsure if the hut was OK.

My wife Jue, quite concerned, asked if the pilots had ejected safely and for several minutes there was some confusion. Her sister was on about a bizarre weather condition that hit and Jue was on about a fighter jet ploughing into the beach!

I live not too many miles away from the North York Moors and on top of there is a well-known air strip at Sutton Bank, mainly used by gliders. I say air strip. It's just a massive flat field and they land pretty much from whatever direction they please, as you do when you've got no engine.

We were doing a job up there one day and had to take the van across the field. It was boggy but I was following a man with flashing lights on his car, so we were in safe hands. I got stuck and a glider nearly took us out, and I'm really not exaggerating when I say we had to duck. The silly twat and his flashing lights nearly got us killed. I shit myself.

The family seem to take my life with a pinch of salt which perhaps is the best thing to do. At tea some nights, sitting round the table, I ask: "Good day at school, boys?" The normal sort of stuff. Sometimes once in a blue moon they may ask if I've had a good day at work and what did I do, and where did I go. Oh, same old same old, nearly got taken out by a glider, someone pulled a gun on me, met the PM, went down a mine, got stuck in a snow drift, talked football with Kevin Keegan, got caught up in a riot, had some bad lads try to put my windscreen through with a baseball bat, was a press conference with a grieving mother whose child had just been murdered.

I don't talk of the heavy death stuff unless they ask or have seen it on TV, and then I just give them the smallest of details. As a parent you do try and protect your children from the shit that goes on in the outside world and I'm no different, even if I cover it. And then you realise they're only buttering you up for a lift back from youth club at 9:30 and really don't give a shit what you did at work that day.

You do develop that police and squaddie sense of humour. I guess it's a coping mechanism because if you were to dwell on things too much it would surely send you mad. Perhaps I'm at that stage in life now. How can it not affect you in some way?

When that Chinook came down on The Mull of Kintyre and 20 or so military intelligence guys, not to mention the crew, lost their lives, I remember being asked what it was like to cover a story with such massive loss of life. I replied: "The seafood up there is fantastic, and the views aren't too bad either."

The guy who asked was horrified at how I could be so bloody flippant. "What am I supposed to do?" I replied. "Put myself in the positions of their wives and children and families and their emotions on hearing the news that their loved ones would never be coming home again. In fact, some bodies couldn't be identified, even from dental records."

Well, mate, let me tell you I cover so much death and destruction and hear such gory details day in and day out it really is unbelievable that I haven't flipped, but I think I'm on the brink.

The day I saw three dead bodies in a car crash and one of them had been decapitated really did put me off my tea that night, but do we ever have anyone ask after our mental well-being? Do we ever get asked if we'd like to talk it over with a health professional? Do we ever get counselling, or told to take a few days off and get over it? Do we fuck!

You get told once you've finished sending the pictures in, there's another job for you in Newcastle. When do you think you'll be there?

I know a cameraman who covered the genocide in Rwanda, a really great guy, but he's not slept for 15 years and there's a few other lads that have covered war zones and seen atrocities that have given them sleepless nights but it never comes out, only to other media lads and after a few beers.

On the subject of crashes, many years ago a small twin-engine plane crashed on take-off at the bottom of the runway at Teesside Airport, now called something completely stupid. We turned up at the airport with the rest of the pack and were filled in with details by their PR guy, a really nice bloke called John Whiting, who would always pull out all the stops for you (PR people take note).

He didn't know much, except the plane was either owned or leased by ICI and that it was en route to France, it had a suspected engine failure and belly flopped to the ground with three or four people on board. There were no casualties. Everyone was shook up and the aircraft was written off.

What he and we weren't told was what it was carrying. At the time I lived quite close to the airport and with our contacts we got there in very quick time, as did everyone else, everyone else that is except the ICI boys. John sorted it out for us to go airside, up the runway and to the crashed plane. Needless to say, the runway was closed with all flights diverted.

The plane indeed was a write-off, but still in one piece and on occasions like this, even before the aircraft investigation board arrive, we became experts and did their job for them. We all agreed it was an engine failure and everyone was lucky to be alive. As we were taking a few shots, this mini bus piled up the runway, horns beeping, lights flashing and arms waving. It came to a screeching halt right in front of us, and out got half a dozen people in full goon suits (those nuclear biological space suits you see in movies), complete with B.A.(breathing apparatus).

To say looks and words were exchanged would be an understatement. The fuckers were waving Geiger counters about and shaking their heads. We were no more than five feet away from the plane, and now realizing that even in the midst of a plane crash, this was most unusual.

Two goons went inside the aircraft and recovered a large steel box. They then got back in their van and disappeared back down the runway. It really was a Dustin Hoffman virus moment. No one, as far as I could see, was going green or foaming at the mouth and the area hadn't been sealed off. It then became like some sort of synchronized swimming event with everyone slowly taking large steps backwards, but all the while looking forwards at the stricken aircraft.

Later at a Press briefing by a somewhat tentative-looking John, it transpired that the box was safe and nothing escaped from it. Well, thank the Lord for that.

"Oh by the way, John, one small little detail, " we asked. "Just exactly what hadn't escaped from the box, that had been in the aircraft, that we had stood five feet away from without an NBC (Nuclear, Biological, Chemical) suit and B.A?"

John had sort of expected this question and had tried to work out some sort of damage limitation reply, but seeing as he was with us, showing us around the plane, he was just as fucked off as we were and just came out with the truth – "Radioactive isotopes!"

Floods

Fortunately, we don't get many natural disasters in this country; the odd mud slide, a bit of snow now and then and occasional large fire is just about it. I did once however nearly get thrown out of bed in a Leeds hotel room due to an earthquake, but it's not like we're living on the Pacific Rim, so we're lucky, compared to some places.

The largest threat by God to our little country is flooding. Although there is generally little loss of life, the consequences on people's homes, lives and businesses is sometimes catastrophic. In the UK, as we all know, it rains and at times it rains a lot, but recently over the past few years the effects of a lot of rain has been untold heartache and destruction.

Looking back, I can't seem to recall it raining any more or any less than it rains now. News desks around the world are fascinated by the weather; it's too hot, it's too cold, it's snowing, it's 15 below, it's the hottest day since records began and so on.

Sky's no different. The first snow falls and all hell breaks loose. Last year, with almost two inches lying on the North York Moors, our helicopter was dispatched. It really is that big a deal for some reason.

And the slightest dusting in London gets the National Guard get called out. More than two days of temperatures in the 80s and we're all going to die of skin cancer. It's the same every year so what should we do? We all look to the Government for reassurance and advice because we're all too thick to work it out for ourselves. If the roads are snowy and icy, don't go on them. If the sun is melting your skin, don't go out in it, but if you have to, wear a sun block and drink lots of fluids. The weather centre people and the AA lads will make sure we all don't die of ignorance.

But the old people, oh my God, the old people, how they will cope? Well, they'll cope as well as they have been coping for, for the past 70, 80 or 90 years. This may come as a shock to some news editors, but in the Summer it sometimes gets hot and in the Winter it sometimes gets cold, and it will probably rain, and it may carry on like this for some time.

It makes me laugh when people come back from ski trips. Do they ever moan that it's been too cold and all the roads have snow on them? Do they return from languishing on a Spanish beach in midsummer and moan it's too hot (well, as Brits, I guess we do), but do the locals ever moan or call for government intervention? No, why not? Because that's just what happens and they get used to it.

So now, if it rains for more than two days solid, there is a very good chance that I'm going to be called out to do flood pictures, and I really don't remember it being like that before. It must be global warming, mustn't it? I really don't know. Global warming must be having some effect and to be fair over the last three or four years there does seem to have been a lot of flooding about, and if it is global warming and if this present trend of flooding continues, then we're already screwed, so there's no point in trying to get the 2018 World Cup played here because we'll all be swimming with the fishes.

It really is frightening though. I have covered flooding in Hull, Carlisle, Toll Bar in Doncaster, North Yorkshire, Cleveland, Northumberland and most recently Cumbria, where as one newspaper put it, it was the perfect storm. That day the missus turns round to me and informs me that I'll be doing flooding this afternoon, as my part-time news editor, she often gets it right. Mind, she's had many years of practice.

So I set off to work covering a routine press conference about a missing woman, thinking the missus had called this one wrong. By lunch time I had still not been diverted onto the big weather story, which made me think some other poor bastard in another part of the country had got it worse and was out there knee deep in shit, bringing the pictures back for you to savour in your nice warm cosy living room, to be watched on your new plasma in HD.

At 4pm, I got the call – Cumbria's under water, go there. I always find it a tad strange that when the shit happens every normal person is trying to get away from harm and danger, and we head towards it. There's a bomb gone off in Warrington – go there! There's a riot in Newcastle – get there as quickly as you can. ICI is on fire in Teesside and about to go up – how quickly can you get some pictures? There's been a toxic leak at a nuclear power station, some bloke's got some hostages and is firing at random – when can you feed your material in?

As with all good newsrooms they want the pictures yesterday, fortunately on that night, the news editor was a guy called Roger Protheroe. A good guy who knows his stuff and indeed his staff, he knew what it's like to be on the road, and valued and trusted your opinion, and a good job he was on, because if Old-Flap-A-Jack had been on, who knows what would have happened.

I headed towards Kendal, where the river was about to breach. The lads on our satellite truck were already there, kicking out live pictures with on-the-spot reports, and things were starting to look bad.

The trip over the Pennines from Teesside was as bad as I have ever experienced. I drove at 20 miles an hour with almost zero visibility and lost count of the times I was nearly blown off the road I had aching wrists due to holding on to the steering wheel so hard, unbelievable. I have never experienced wind and rain like that ever, wipers constantly on full belt, and the rain hitting the ground so hard, both vertically and horizontally, that the road just kept on disappearing.

At least I wasn't on some dodgy A road going over the Pennines in the dark at 2000ft with zero visibility with steep drops to a certain death on every corner. Oh that's right, I was, yes I was. Did I ever get any thanks for it, did we ever get any thanks for it? Apart from Roger, not a word, and the night had only just begun. If ever a job was literally going to kill me this would be it. Really I mean that, and I've had a few close shaves.

Having got to Kendal, we were rerouted to Cockermouth, where by all accounts the shit really had hit the fan. I had now been driving for over seven hours and on the back of a normal day, I was knackered, the concentration had sapped just about all the energy I had left out of me and as we all know, that's when things happen.

Cockermouth had been on my sat nav for several hours and at times I was only a few miles away but every road I tried was flooded out. Cars were abandoned left, right and centre; some subsequently washed away.

A police officer had been swept to his death in nearby Workington when a bridge gave way as he was stopping members of the public from using it. The night really had the possibility of turning into the Big One – that's news speak for incidents along the lines of Lockerbie, Hillsborough and Bradford; unprecedented occasions with sadly a large loss of life. What if a tourist bus was on that bridge, or any bridge? The consequences just weren't worth thinking about. Losing one life was bad enough, and, in my view the guy was a hero; all the emergency services are, and indeed they were again that night.

At half past eleven I managed to get a phone signal, and rang Roger. I had no choice but to bail out, I just couldn't physically get there. I was beat. I rang Lobel on our Sat truck to find out how he was doing, and to my disbelief he told me along with Spinney, Shearsy and Mike, they were in the centre of Cockermouth, and that the only people who couldn't make it into Cockermouth that night were the BBC and wankers!

The gauntlet had been thrown down. I was just going to have to walk in. No ifs, no buts, I wasn't missing out on this one, a once in a thousand year occasion they called it. God knows how I managed it but I did get there in the end, somehow. Technically I was the first crew in there, but Spinney and Shearsy had been banging off shots with the live camera for 20 minutes before my arrival, so when I turned up they put Mike live on air and I went news gathering.

Conditions were still terrible. It was like trying to shoot whilst standing under a shower; water on the lens, water in the view finder, water on my glasses. I had no idea what I was shooting or what it would look like. It was all guess work. Events like this always seem so surreal. You hear it all the time when people get interviewed after some disaster. They say it was just like something out of the movies. It takes a while to get your head round what you witness.

Two Sea King helicopters were hovering overhead, rotor blades popping, their searchlights blinding you for split seconds at a time. You could feel the down blast as they lifted people off the roofs and out of windows, and they were low, very low. Police and fire crews' radios were crackling and sirens wailing. It was full on.

I ran towards the centre of town just a few streets from where we were broadcasting live, and the sight I saw was very surreal. A helicopter was directly above me and in front of me was a speed boat full of fire crew going up and down the high street in ten feet of water, shooting rapids. I'd never seen that before.

Really it was just like they do on the Colorado river and as fierce as their rapids to boot, but this wasn't the Colorado river, but a quite little high street in a sleepy little market town in Cumbria. You really were expecting Spielberg to step out of the shadows and shout, "Cut!" but this was no movie set. This was for real, and dangling above us on winches were real people being saved and taken to safety.

People were risking their lives and people's lives were being saved. You never get the full 360 degree picture – the noise, sweat, nerves and adrenaline – when you watch it on the telly, but we really do try to capture the atmosphere as well as the action. And like a fool I was in at the deep end, a wall of water had just washed over my waders and now my legs were stuck like lead.

You should never, ever, ever wade into water, in situations like this; one manhole or drain cover that's off and down you go. Who knows what else lies below the muddy water, electric cables, barbed wire, anything could be waiting for you. I had just broken a golden rule to get the shot, and shook myself up a bit. No shot is worth your life. I quickly scrambled back out of the drink, counting my lucky stars, and vowing to myself that never again would I let a situation get the better of me.

The night wore on and I believe the viewing figures went through the roof. You all like a good disaster, especially when you can watch it unfold live on TV. It's sad human nature. It's like looking at a car crash; it's sick to do but interesting. I myself stopped looking at shit like that. I have seen enough death and carnage over the years and certainly don't want those pictures burnt into my memory to carry around for years to come.

I don't know why but looking down a lens seems to divorce you from reality, but it was hard to be anything but involved at Cockermouth. We found a hotel and got to the bar at about 4ish. It was shut but we opened it, and all tried to calm down and unwind, but it's impossible with so much adrenaline still buzzing about. I did manage a few hours' sleep before the full horror of the flooding was brought to sight as daylight broke.

It was hard enough to get back into the centre. Bridges that we used in the night had just gone. We were lucky boys, I guess. The power and force of water was astonishing. Cars were swept away; windows, garage doors, and gardens all washed away – utter destruction.

We jumped a police cordon and got right to the scene. People were still being rescued; pets were lost or stranded; people's business and livelihoods had just been washed away. We spoke to many people and everyone had a story to tell.

A young couple had just finished doing up their house. The water line was 8ft up their living room wall. Everything gone, it was ruined, but it could all be replaced. They really did feel lucky to be alive. A lot of people were uninsured and lost everything. Photos and wedding albums were strewn down the streets, videos of the kids when they were babies ruined, memories lost forever; bank details, birth certificates, cheques books, credit cards – everything gone.

People had that complete helpless look about them and walked around like empty shells. Many were in tears, and many more were just numb. Where do you start to rebuild your life after that? In Toll Bar it was some two years after the flooding that everyone had moved completely back in.

No one living near a river or where there have been floods before can get insurance these days. It's not that they can't afford it, but the insurance companies just aren't interested. To be fair over the last few years they really have had their fingers burnt with flood claims, so people living near water are not generally insured, so therefore they can't sell their houses, and so it goes on.

As we moved around the streets I noticed a tiny little fish lying on the ground, flapping about on its last legs, helpless. It was a small gesture but we put it back in the water and it swam away. If this sort of flooding is what lies ahead, and global warming is to blame then within my lifetime a flood of biblical proportions will indeed wipe out a town, village or even a city with monumental loss of life.

I'm not Nostradamus. I'm just a cameraman, but I can see what's happening and it's time to wake up and smell the coffee, and give our grandchildren a fighting chance.

Sometime later I was told we won some sort of gong for that night's coverage. I am still waiting for it!

UFOs

The boys and Jue bought me a tent, great! The only up side I see in camping and living in the great outdoors is the fact you have to consume large amounts of alcohol to sleep at night, and when it rains, which it does a lot in this country, then camping really does become fun.

To be fair I love it most of the time, apart from putting the tent up and taking it down and a few bits in-between, it's brilliant. Everyone should try it, at least once. We normally go camping with Baz and his family. Our kids think it's some sort of Bushtucker Trial, living off the land. What with those wild pizzas, curries and fish and chips, we don't have to set too many traps.

My tent is so big you could quite easily get a car in there. I kid you not. It's the size of those ones you saw Gaddafi holding summits in, in the middle of the desert, but without the camels, and the en-suite is nearly 300 yards away.

We have found the best campsite in the UK, namely Bainbridge Ings at Hawes in the Yorkshire Dales. It's run by Mark and Janet – a lovely couple. This place is great for many reasons.

Firstly it set up high on a hillside (therefore not many mozzies, the wind blows them away) and secondly it is surrounded by some of the greatest views that the Dales have to offer. You're never cramped in or feel claustrophobic as the tents and campervans are pitched around a field that you could quite happily play a World Cup qualifier in, and indeed on more than one occasion we have.

Another great feature with being so high up is the fact that you actually look down on the aircraft that the RAF lads train in. Straight up, you can see them coming up the valley or the dale to be more precise, flying at pretty much zero feet. It's not uncommon to actually duck as they come over. As for the helicopters – well you might get a glimpse of one or two but they are so low the dry stone walls just hide them. It defies belief of these lads' flying capabilities.

But the very best thing about camping and being outdoors in Hawes is the fact it's great for UFO spotting. Honestly, the little buggers buzz our tent most nights. This place is the sort of location Spielberg could shoot Close Encounters of the Third Kind '2' in. If he's already done 2, he could shoot 3 there.

Late at night when it's quiet, with no wind, and all you can hear in the distance is the faint clatter of happy campers and the odd sheep baa-ing from across the dale, it's amazing to look up at the night sky. If you're lucky enough to have no cloud cover, you will see a fantastic starry night, void of any light pollution. You would think you were in an observatory or planetarium. You can, with a little effort, actually touch the stars, so you get the picture. There seems to be a shooting star every 30 seconds, and with the naked eye it is even possible to see satellites and even the International space station the odd time it passes over head.

Therefore it is almost inevitable you will see UFOs or indeed be captured by them or have alien implants put in your body, and possibly lose not only hours but days at a time, which Baz and I often do, after some of the sessions we've had there over the years.

Anyway this one night, standing round the BBQ, about 9.30 ish, getting on for late dusk and last light, we noticed some "alien activity". It was witnessed by at least 20 people in five or six tents. What we saw was a very extraordinary bright light across the valley, just up the fell from a place called Hardraw, which you could see quite clearly through the binoculars, even in the dim light. (Obviously the mother ship).

At the point of just about burning all the sausages and burgers, we then noticed the light changing colour and landing. It was now red and sort of pulsing and turning back whitish.

We were several miles away and we know there are a couple of steep roads across the hills in that general direction and you see headlights and brake lights all the time in the darkness, but this now red light seemed bigger than any brakelight and we were pretty certain it was off-road. A fire perhaps, no, flare, no, search lights maybe, no.

We have between us some 50 odd years in the TV business and have heard most tales and tall stories over the decades, but there we were with possibly one of our own that no one in their right mind would believe. As we were just at the "Who do we sell this story to?" stage, the now white pulsing light started going vertical. We considered a helicopter, Army night manoeuvres, and went back to burning dead animals on the barbie.

"Baz, if it's a helicopter, then how come it's doing that?" I asked, as out of the big red and white pulsating light came a stream of smaller red ones – three in all, the same distance apart, also heading vertically.

As two experienced cameramen, it was obvious one of us would have a camera to hand, but looking through the view finder of a small stills camera you could see nothing. It was too dark. Even with our DV cameras, we got the same result.

Cameras like light and by now there wasn't any or at least very little. Even if we had had our professional cameras with us and used a setting on them which is something akin to night vision, we still probably would have got very little. Maybe a small red blob that certainly wouldn't stand up to cross examination in a court of law, that indeed these pictures were the smoking gun that proved beyond all reasonable doubt that there were UFOs, piloted by aliens from another planet.

Seconds later, another four red lights appeared out of the mother ship, seven red lights in all now – a chain of three, then a chain of 4, all glowing and pulsing red/white, heading vertically. There were gasps from the tent next door and everyone in and around the campsite were been summoned to the show.

It was electric. Tongues were wagging, kids were shouting, my sausages were burning, people were shouting out for cameras and a very strange thing was happening – it was truly amazing.

Then another two red orbs appeared, so now there were nine red and white lights, one large mother ship, and many excited people. There was an atmosphere you could cut with a knife; indeed you could taste it.

Were these really, really UFOs? Am I really looking at objects from another world? Fucking hell! Is this it? Is this really it? Yes I was pissed, and so was Baz. In fact, most of the campsite was pretty bevvied up! Was this some sort of massive illusion or some kind of shock hypnosis that stage magicians use? Or was this the real McCoy and were these indeed UFOs that we were seeing?

God, I was so excited and amazed and I guess shocked, but not frightened just intrigued.

"Fuck Baz, what if they're, like, actually really invading?" I said.

What a bizarre thought. War of the Worlds comes to Hawes! But it was for real, and all I had to defend myself and my family was a pair of barbeque tongs and pretty shit ones at that.

The UFOs, and I will call them UFOs, were by now all at different altitudes and distances. Some now seemed to disappear, as though the lights were being switched off (and no they were definitely not lanterns).

Others were shooting off at monumental speed, leaving a coloured sort of vapour trail. They were heading either North or West or East, so the prevailing winds had no input then.

Then they were gone. The mother ship just disappeared. We didn't see it take back off. I guess they turned it invisible, left it where it was, took on human appearances and took off for a night on the piss in Hawes, or something like that.

It was indeed the story of the holiday, better than any Discovery Channel UFO documentary, and will stay with me for the rest of my life.

Those boys of the Wensleydale and District UFO Acrobatic Team sure know how to put on a good show! Jue, needless to say, never saw anything as she was in the loo! She didn't believe a word anyone said to her, not even our boys. She thought it was a wind-up. If even my wife was sceptical, what would the non-believers say? Well bollocks to what they would say! We know what we saw, and what we saw didn't come from our planet. Fact.

It's not the first time that Baz and I have encountered objects from another world. Again on another brilliant starry night high above the fells we saw a perfect triangle of very bright stars. We were trying to work out what constellation we were looking at through Baz's new app on his new iphone, when at the same time and at the same second they all took off at speed in different directions. We decided there and then not to tell anyone about this incident. What was the point? No one would believe us (again), but we are absolutely sure our little fellas from afar, know damn well that we are seeing them, and they're having a bit of a laugh at our expense.

Ask any local living in the Dales and without exception at one time or another they will tell you they have seen things that they can't or won't explain. But what our alien chums don't know is, next time we go camping at Hawes, we're planning on catching one and wiping the smiles off a lot of people's faces. All we need now is a cunning plan.

And Finally

After 45 Years on this planet I have finally worked out what life's all about, and unlike in the Hitch Hikers Gide to the Galaxy it's not 43, or was that 47, no it's about being happy and healthy, for myself and the missus, but mainly for my kids. If you go through life being happy and healthy then I guess you've had a good life, being happy and healthy and a mass murderer to boot does not count. If you can go to work with a smile on your face knowing your family are safe and well then nothing else really matters, let's face it the bills always get paid, most of the time.

I am very lucky and very content, of course shit happens but it's how you deal with it, and dealing with it well makes you a better and stronger person, I'm starting to sound like the Dalai Lama, in fact having read a few books on Buddhism there's a lot to be said for the religion. I have tried to adopt some of its mantras such as being happy, treating other people well and having no negative thoughts. It lasted about 20 minutes before someone cut me up on the motorway and I wanted to rip their bloody head off. It seems impossible to adapt any happy self respecting religion in this greedy fast Western Society when everyone wants things yesterday and life's all about making a fast buck. I have tried to put myself in other people's situations and not slag anyone off, but in the TV industry this again is almost impossible, and over the years I have been screwed over many times, so therefore you must learn to play the game. Today I am more relaxed and less stressed and more tolerant of people. I do know a great many people and there isn't a press conference in the North that I don't know someone at, if not most. I get the impression that I'm liked, but who knows you'll have to ask them. I have few genuine close friends out of choice, and believe it or not I'm a very private person, so God knows why I'm writing this book, but I feel some of the stories are quite revealing and my past experiences and remembering people and episodes from years gone by has brought a real smile to my face.

The future is bright, to start with I still have a job, and Sky News is at the cutting edge of the news industry so that will keep me on my toes, most of the time. I love to watch my kids grow up, and play badminton, football and do all the daddy things you do with them before they rob you blind and disappear into the big wild world. At mid teens I see them turning into young men, in fact my relationship with my kids is so good that at times they even talk to me. My wife Jue has been at my side since we met at 15 as teenage sweethearts and has never left, she knows when she's onto a good thing, but seriously though she understands me better than anyone, to the degree that one look will tell her what mood I'm in. She's the level headed one in the family, the one that thinks for us all before we jump and I'm very lucky to have her. We all make mistakes and do things we regret, and I just hope she never finds out about them (joke), but me and the boys are very lucky and one day they will understand this, and we love her to bits.

Have you ever thought or planned your perfect day? Do it now, then carry it out, mine is get up, as you do, drop the boys off at school and college, go for a swim, walk the dog on the beach, meet ten bellies (Baz) in Charlie Chalks for a beer, come back spark the barby, have it ready for when the boys get back and then watch a movie together or in the summer go over the park for a game of cricket. I have many perfect days only spoiled by too much Stella in Charlie Chalks. Jue's allowed to do everything as well, except come for a beer or touch my BBQ or indeed play cricket as she has zero coordination, but sometimes she's allowed to bat, we have now all agreed to stop bowling bouncers at her!

I also lead a double life as an artist. One day Jue came back with some paints and a canvas, having looked for ages to hang something above our fireplace she decided that what she had seen was crap and that I could do better and with me having an O'Level in Art, she was right.

That was a few years ago and I have created over a hundred and forty masterpieces and got bitten by the bug almost to the stage of obsession. Some times when I'm off shift I stay up all night and paint two or three pieces; other times I would jump out of bed at two in the morning put some Led Zepp on and paint till the sun comes up.

I started reading up on Kandinsky, Monet, Pollock and David Hockney I looked deeply at the work of Emin and Hurst, I got anal about the whole thing, and still am.

I really discovered a whole new world, and still get so excited before I paint one that I feel like a little kid who knows he's getting his first bike off Santa for Christmas.

Always abstract, but experimenting and improvising all the time. I have spent thousands on paint and canvasses and love everyone I have ever done, I have used hairdryers, eggcups, chop sticks, knives and folks to get different effects and expand my techniques, I have baked canvas and put paints in the microwave to get just the right consistency and texture, I have spent days just looking at a blank canvas and played with ideas in my head, I really have started to look at things differently Trees, Parks, Beaches,

People, Stars, The Moon and beyond have all in some way made it onto canvas. Even walking the dog around the park after a wet evening when the following day the paths are drying out I can see shapes on the damp tarmac. One day I was attacked by a thing, I have no idea what it was, to me it was just a thing, I rushed home and cracked open the paint and put it down on canvas.

The burning question was and still is to a certain extent, what I am I going to do with all this work? I believe in myself and know that it's good enough to exhibit, so now what? The family and some chums laughed when I told them I would find the masses and make a name for myself, I'll show you, they don't call me Dick Willington for nothing.

I got my break from a lovely lady called Carol who owned an Art Gallery in nearby Yarm, a small North Yorkshire Market Town, cobbled streets and all that, one day having chewed the idea over of showing some work with ten bellies in the Black Bull down there, I then walked into her gallery and asked her for an exhibition, she thought it was a drunken prank, so the next day I took a few paintings down and she kindly let me put them on her walls, I also got some people to go down there and write down in a book their true full comments, it was all very positive in fact it was better than that, Carol offered me my first full blown exhibition, and for that I will forever be truly great full to her. Thanks once again. I was absolutely buzzing I had just won the Pools, Lotto and Euro Millions all at the same time.

One night about 1 in the morning just before the opening of my exhibition, I was coming back from a job and stopped outside the gallery, my work was being displayed in the front windows and looked absolutely awesome, a little tear ran down my face. I felt so proud, I had proved everyone wrong, I had done it.

I was having an exhibition, people strangers were going to look at my work and judge it, it was there for all to see, I had made it happen, I knew my work was good enough to show and show it I did.

Let me rewind a few months before the greatest Art exhibition ever seen. I needed a gimmick, something to publicise the event, some way of getting the media down to cover the event, I know all the local media lads and lasses, but they wouldn't publicise some exhibition by some unknown artist on their nightly TV programs without a gimmick. I needed to do something big, something unusual, and something that would get tongues wagging, something that had never been done before, something that's completely out of the ordinary and bizarre. So I did, I hired Ann.

Ann is a 4 ½ tonne Asian Elephant and I walked her down Yarm High Street to my exhibition. She did the trick. I won't bore you with the details of how it happened but suffice to say it's the only time in my life I have been physically sick with worry. An hour before the event I still wasn't 100% sure she was going to turn up, and outside the gallery were a lot of people and a lot of media, but she did, check it out on the website. It was a truly amazing day and the experience will remain with me forever. Even the wankers that thought it was cruel didn't get me down.

She was born in captivity and retired from the circus, she is owned and loved by the people that keep her. That's her life, it's the only one she knows, she costs a fortune to look after with feeding, heating and vet bills to pay for and as far as I was concerned I was helping to pay for her upkeep and wellbeing. For her side of the bargain she had to give me 15 minutes and walk a few hundred yards up a street.

I had got the local school kids down for the event of which few had seen a live Elephant, and if not for Ann walking down the High Street many would probably never see one at all.

She inspired many, what a truly wonderful animal, and when she looked at you she looked straight into your eyes, you don't get that on the Discovery Channel. I felt privileged to walk with her and will defend my decision to hire her to the hilt. Needless to say she completely overshadowed the entire exhibition, but who cares. I got the publicity I was after and am now world famous in Eaglescliffe, and my work is selling like hot cakes, so get in quick cos this time next year they'll be worth millions.

Hopefully by the time you read this my little pet project will have come to fruition, and that is entering the world of big business, selling Fairies, yes that's right Fairies I know some people think it's cruel but if It can make me a buck or two and I can get away with it I will.

Let me briefly explain, some time ago Jue was moaning on about the amount of washing she was doing, saying stuff like she does vast amounts every day and where does it all come from and wouldn't it be nice if one day I went hunting for the washing machine which is hidden somewhere in the kitchen and perhaps have a little go myself, and then again hunt round for an iron and ironing board and maybe have a whack at that as well, and when it's all done and dusted put it all away again, (a very frightening thought, indeed to me a dangerous one), so I suggested to her that what she needed was a Washing Fairy to do it all for her, the idea from then on snowballed, get some Fairies, put them in a can, and when the can is opened and the fairy released they will grant you one wish for releasing them, so I bought a whole job lot of Fairies off an old ogre.

So now we have a washing fairy to do the washing, a cooking

fairy to do the cooking, a fishing fairy that guarantees you will catch the biggest fish ever, a golfing fairy that guarantees you will get a hole in one, a slimming fairy, a homework fairy, a gardening fairy, a shopping fairy, etc, etc you get the picture, there's loads of them so check out the web site. The cans do carry a disclaimer mind.

It's all got a bit spooky, really. I gave a lot of cans to friends and people I know to get some feedback, and whether this is a mass wind up or not I don't know, but people are actually telling me that some wishes they made really came true. A nameless guy I gave one to reckons the 2 grand he won on a scratch card was only because he gave the magic can a shake. His missus doesn't know of his little bit of good fortune, but that business trip he went on recently was actually a stag do, so who knows, give it a whirl, maybe there are good forces at work here.

So there you have it, yes I paint and act and take photos and now write and have entered the business world, so watch out Sir Alan and you Dragons I'm hot on your heels. I have no idea if any of this will ever come to anything, I don't really care, I've enjoyed doing it and if in the years to come when my kids grow up and my grandchildren wonder just what was mad Granddad Karl like, they may well have a read of this book I've written and realize that yes, he was indeed truly as mad as a basket of badgers, but keen to give anything a go, but also happy and healthy and loved his family dearly, and lived life to the full.

LUV Karl.xxxxxx

Check out www.karlcoatesart.com

And also www.themagicfairycompany.com

On Facebook, find me at Karl Coates and karlcoatesart.com

Follow me on Twitter @ CameramanArtist

And Now for Some Big Hugs and Thank Yous

There are a lot of people who I would like to give a mention to either for their help in writing this epic, or for their ideas and memories or their support and wisdom, especially the lads that gave me the photos and told me there would be no copyright issues(I have it in writing). Also big hugs to all those I have worked with, and enjoy being around.

So a big thank you to: Christine Fieldhouse, who deciphered all the crap I gave her and made it make sense, Baz (Freelance) luv ya, Jonny (BBC), Les (BBC) for getting me started, Jue and the boys, Jordan and Kieran, for all their love and support, Mum, and all the support from my wider family. The boys at my local Gazette, all the lads at North News And Pictures, Ted Ditchburn, Raoul Dixon, Richard, Kev, Will, Craig, Paul Kingston and the rest of the team, Keith Perry (the Sun), John Giles, Own Humphreys (Press Association), Eddie Robson, Shaun Johnson (BBC) mate and drinking buddy, Stu Bolton and Co (Northern Echo), Joe, The Caine Cartel, Gary, Pete and Dave, truly outstanding drinkers and not bad cameramen either, Malik Walton (BBC), Frazer (the batsman) Maude, Scott and Brian Heppel (the best freelance snappers on the planet), Reevie, Whincup (BBC), just for amusing me, Crossy, Nobby (BBC), Gareth, Tommo, Phil Spence (Daily Mirror).

Big hugs also go to Jean Logan, Dr's Kumar, Stockley, Smith and Ellinger for helping me out with my little problems, Ta, you saved my life.

And now massive hugs and kisses for everyone at Sky News, especially Lynn Hobbs (thanks Lynn. x), Mark Lobel, Shearsy (Steptoe and son, the funniest guys on the road and great mates, beware when they're about), Jackie, Rodger, Simon, Martin Brunt, Dovver's, Chris, Ronnie, Ray, James, Jane, Andy D, Andy N, Mike, Tom, Crabbers, Richie, Francis, Me old mucker Mr Hunter, Len, me old bosses, Nick Pollard, Chris Hampson, Coley and everyone else, but mainly big hugs to all the lads and lasses in the field, whatever situation you find yourselves in, in whatever part of the world, keep safe. X

I know I must have missed a whole bunch of people out that I should have given a mention to, I'm sorry, please don't give me a hard time when you see me, I'll take you for a beer and curry instead.

And Finally Finally Finally

We all have a book in us as they say however perhaps not a whole book, so now for my next trick, I am in the process of putting book number two together and would love to hear from anyone in the news gathering industry, past or present that has a good story to tell. (Cameramen, Reporters, Presenters, Producers, Snappers, Fixers, Paper Hacks, Paparazzi, Sat Engineers, Radio boys, Directors, Gallery Lads, News Paper Editors, Freelancers), any one at all, I guess the Sports lads can be included as well.

Give me your best funniest story, Try and leave all the death and destruction out of it but if it's relevant then put it in, and I'll stick the best ones in a book and make you all millions. There's no excuses, if I can write a book, then I'm pretty sure everyone out there in media land can knock out 1 or 2 thousand words, more or less if you like, that's only about 4 pages or so.

If you've never put pen to paper since school then do it now, grab a few tinnes or a bottle of plonk and start scribbling, you've got nothing to lose, I know most cameramen and snappers can barely read or write, me included, but there's no excuse, cos I know you all have word check on your computer, so do it.

Come on, Paxman, Kate Adie, Jeremy Thompson, Mark Austin, Jon Snow and the like, give us all a laugh. It will without doubt be the greatest book ever published (well almost). I am hopefully going to do a similar sort of thing with the US media and stick all their crazy and bizarre stories in a book, that really will be some read, JFK, Area 51, Roswell, Marilyn, Nixon, Big foot etc, all from the people that were actually there, will wait and see if it takes off, no doubt some bastard reading this will nick my idea, make millions and become an international celeb.

The deal is this, 50% of the profits(if it makes any) will be shared equally amongst the contributors, I suspect that will equate to something like 3.5 million per person (joke), with royalties for life, that bit will be true, 25% of the profits go to me as that's only fair cos I'm skint and it's my idea and I'm doing the donkey work putting it together, and the other 25% will go to Diabetes UK, as several years ago my eldest son was diagnosed with type 1 diabetes, a life changing condition that affects not just him but the entire family. It's a good cause and it feels good to do your bit, and one day like cancer they may well find a cure, but only if they have enough cash to do the research.

There you have it, go and write me a book, you can find my email address on my web site, or Google me as they say, please give a short I.D of yourself, who you work for, what you do, where the story took place, etc, but make it short, and am not interested in how many O levels you've got, or what you drive, just give me the facts dear boy/girl. Also a picture would be good, an action one preferably if not then any old mug shot will do. Together we can do this and make it work, not just for charity, not just for you and the satisfaction that you are indeed in print, but mainly and most importantly for ME.

Karl.xxxxx

Beneath the Sky

"Come on Coatesy give us some goss what's it really like at Sky"?

In the desert of New Mexico, just outside of Roswell lies a place that is so Top Secret that until only recently the authorities have confirmed its existence, that place is Area 51, and this my friends is my Area 51 or chapter 34 to more precise, and I am about to blow the lid on the workings and behind the scenes of one of the world's top news rooms, a full blown kiss and tell of who did what to who, who got caught doing things they shouldn't, what really happens out in the field, and stuff that would indeed make the Spartan hairs on Lord Justices Leveson's head stand on end, not to mention me being brought before a Judge and Jury with a possible prison sentence hanging over my head, this chapter could indeed bring not just Sky News but the Entire Murdoch Empire come crashing down, but I have a tale to tell and tell it I must, what I am about to divulge is the truth the whole truth and nothing but the truth, so help me God, so here goes... on the other hand you may find it extremely boring... so I won't bother. X

My legal representatives want me to point out that all of the above is bollocks, absolute bollocks and nothing but bollocks, Sky News or anyone or anything to do with them or Mr Murdoch or anyone or anything has never broken the Law or told Porkies or done anything wrong... ever... at all... ever... OK, so let's just get that straight. Life moves on and I have now left Sky News. But for anyone that wants to get into the industry, there really is only one News Channel that is head and shoulders above all others and that is Sky News. Sorry Beeb, but you run a close second.

Love and best wishes to all.

Karl x